4/2012   OCT 1 8 2006   HU

HISTORY OF WEST AFRICA

THE DIAGRAM GROUP

Facts On File, Inc.

History of Africa: History of West Africa

Copyright © 2003 by The Diagram Group

Diagram Visual Information Ltd

Editorial director:	Denis Kennedy
Editor:	Peter Harrison
Contributor:	Bridget Giles
Consultant:	Keith Lye
Indexer:	Martin Hargreaves
Senior designer:	Lee Lawrence
Designers:	Claire Bojczuk, Christian Owens
Illustrators:	Kathy McDougall, Graham Rosewarne
Research:	Neil McKenna, Patricia Robertson

Library of Congress Cataloging-in-Publication Data
History of West Africa / The Diagram Group.
    p.cm.–(History of Africa)
  Includes bibliographical references and index.
  ISBN 0-8160-5060-0-(set) – ISBN 0-8160-5062-7
    1. Africa, West–History–Miscellanea. I. Diagram Group. II. Series.

DT475. H575 2003
966–dc21   2002035200

Contents

© DIAGRAM

FOREWORD

The six-volume History of Africa series has been designed as a companion set to the Peoples of Africa series. Although, of necessity, there is some overlap between the two series, there is also a significant shift in focus. Whereas Peoples of Africa focuses on ethnographic issues, that is the individual human societies which make up the continent, History of Africa graphically presents a historical overview of the political forces that shape the continent today.

History of West Africa starts off with a description of the region in depth, including its religions, land, climate, and the languages spoken there today, with particular relevance to the colonial legacy as it affected the spoken word region-by-region. There then follows an overview of events from prehistory to the present day, and a brief discussion of the historical sources, such as travelers' tales, that help us to learn about the past.

The major part of the book comprises an in-depth examination of the history of the region from the first humans through the early civilizations or chiefdoms; the development of trade with other countries; the arrival of European colonists, and the effect this had on the indigenous peoples; the struggles for independence in the last century; and the current political situation in the nation, or island, states, in the new millennium.

Interspersed throughout the main text of the book are special features on a variety of political topics or historical themes which bring the region to life, such as the Igbo-Ukwu culture, the Seven True Towns, the Amazons of Dahomey, Fulani *jihads*, and the Women's War, 1929.

Throughout the book the reader will find timelines which list major events; and also maps, diagrams and illustrations, presented in two color throughout, which help to explain these events in more detail, and place them within the context of world events.

Finally, there is a glossary which defines unfamiliar words used within the book, a bibliography, and a comprehensive index.

Taken together with the other five volumes in this series, *History of West Africa* will provide the reader with a memorable snapshot of Africa as a continent with a rich history.

Dates

In this book we use the dating system BCE – Before Common Era – and CE – Common Era. 1 CE is the same year as 1 AD. We have used this system to cater for different religions and beliefs which do not recognize a Christian-based dating system.

The religions of West Africa

The two most widely-practiced religions in West Africa are Islam and Christianity. At least 900 years ago, Islam was introduced from North Africa, primarily as a result of trading across the Sahara. In the 19th century, Christianity was brought to West Africa by European missionaries. Today many Christians and Muslims in West Africa combine the beliefs and practices of an African religion with their belief in Islam or Christianity.

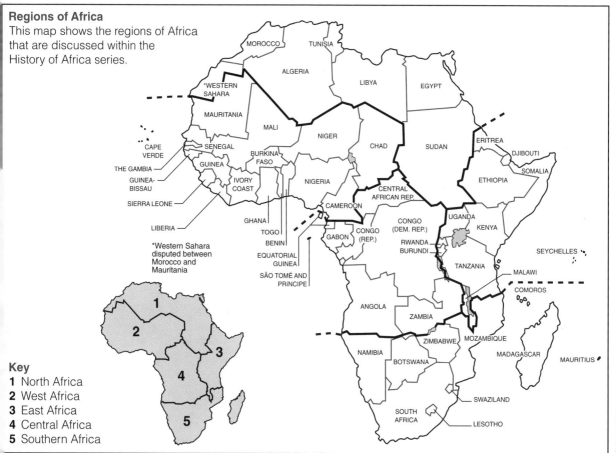

Regions of Africa
This map shows the regions of Africa that are discussed within the History of Africa series.

*Western Sahara disputed between Morocco and Mauritania

Key
1 North Africa
2 West Africa
3 East Africa
4 Central Africa
5 Southern Africa

© DIAGRAM

5

Land

West Africa is a vast region, occupying nearly one-quarter of the African continent. It consists of eighteen countries: Benin, Burkina Faso, Cameroon, Chad, Ivory Coast, Gambia, Ghana, Guinea, Guinea-Bissau, Liberia, Mali, Mauritania, Niger, Nigeria, Senegal, Sierra Leone, Togo, and the island nation of Cape Verde.

The huge, burning Sahara forms the northern part of West Africa. Farther south lies another great semidesert – the Sahel. The Atlantic Ocean lies to the west and south, and the highlands of Cameroon form the southeast border. West Africa is divided into three main areas. Most of West Africa is flat, although the region stands well above sea level, and consists of plateaus more than 600 ft (180 m) high. In some places, rocky hills, known as *inselbergs*, rise up like islands from the plateaus. There are mountainous highlands in the north and west. The highest peaks are volcanic, including Mount Cameroon, which at 13,451 ft (4,100 m) high is the tallest mountain in the region. Coastal lowlands border the Atlantic Ocean, forming a low plain, which gives way to steeper land farther inland.

A number of rivers cut into the mountains. They include the Niger, West Africa's longest river, and the third longest in Africa, which forms a delta where it meets the sea. West Africa also contains Lake Chad, one of the world's largest and shallowest natural lakes.

Flat land above 600 ft

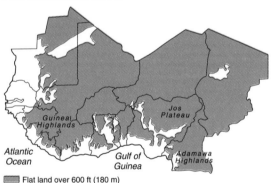

Flat land over 600 ft (180 m)

Mountains above 4,500 ft

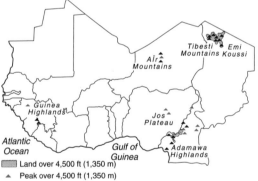

Land over 4,500 ft (1,350 m)
▲ Peak over 4,500 ft (1,350 m)
▲ Peak over 6,000 ft (1,800 m)

Rivers and lakes

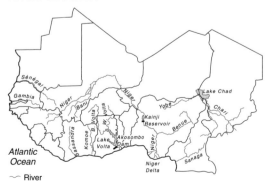

∼ River

Coastal lowlands

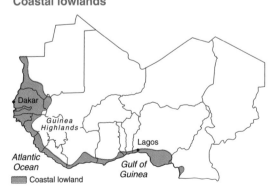

Coastal lowland

Climate

West Africa is almost entirely within the tropics and its climate is mostly hot. Much of the region has distinct wet and dry seasons apart from the semiarid region of the southern Sahara where there is little or no rain.

Temperatures in the Sahara fluctuate enormously from a night-time low of 4 °C (39 °F) to soaring daytime temperatures of above 43 °C (109 °F). Elsewhere temperature ranges are far less extreme. For example, in Dakar, on the Senegal coast, they average between 21° and 28 °C (70° to 82 °F). Inland they vary according to season.

Average rainfall varies enormously. Less than 1 in (2.5 cm) falls in southern Sahara. By contrast, 33 ft (10 m) rain falls annually in the wettest parts of Cameroon.

Temperature (January)

Minimum

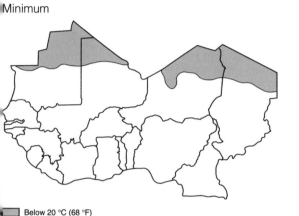

Below 20 °C (68 °F)

Temperature (July)

Maximum

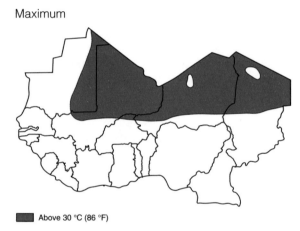

Above 30 °C (86 °F)

Rainfall (November–April)

Maximum

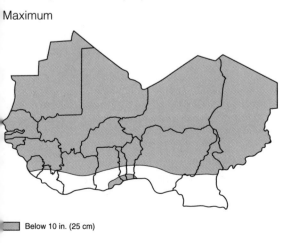

Below 10 in. (25 cm)

Rainfall (May–October)

Minimum

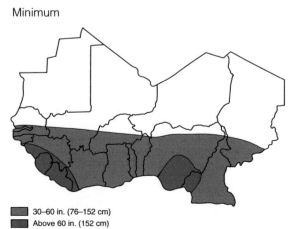

30–60 in. (76–152 cm)
Above 60 in. (152 cm)

© DIAGRAM

7

Benin achieved independence from France in 1960. In 1972 a coup brought Ahmed Kérékou to power, and, in 1975, he declared a one-party communist state. The government abandoned communism in 1989 and, in 1990, democracy was restored.

Burkina Faso became independent in 1960. The army took control in 1966, and multiparty elections took place in 1977. In the 1990s there were attempts to stabilize the country's economy and politics but it remains one of the world's poorest countries.

Cameroon achieved independence in 1960. Since 1960, Cameroon has only had two presidents: Ahmadou Ahidjo, who was president from 1960 until 1982, and Paul Biya, who succeeded him.

Cape Verde achieved independence from Portugal in 1975. Plans to form a federation with Guinea-Bissau were dropped in 1980. The first multiparty elections took place in 1991.

Chad became independent in 1960. The country is politically unstable and has experienced civil war almost continuously since the 1960s. It was a one-party state for many years until democracy was restored in 1996.

Gambia, The became independent in 1965, and a republic in 1970. Between 1982 and 1989, Gambia and Senegal formed a confederation, and tourism was developed. In 1994 a bloodless coup brought Yaha Jammeh to power. He was reelected in 2001.

Ghana gained independence in 1957, and became a one-party state in 1964. In 1991 it returned to multiparty democracy and Jerry Rawlings, who had seized power in 1981, was elected president.

Guinea became independent in 1958 with socialist Sékou Touré as president. He died in 1984 and military rule, under Lansana Conté, was established. A multiparty constitution was introduced in 1991.

Guinea-Bissau became independent in 1974. A series of coups took place and, until 1991, Guinea-Bissau was a one-party state. Multiparty elections took place in 1994, but the country remains poor.

Ivory Coast became independent in 1960. In the 1970s, it was regarded as one of Africa's most stable states, but economic problems mounted. A military coup occurred in 1999. Civilian rule was rapidly restored, but a civil war broke out in 2002.

Liberia became an independent country in 1847. Since the 1980s the country has been politically unstable. Civil war, which first broke out in 1989, has shattered the economy.

Mali became an independent republic in 1960, and a one-party state linked to the Communist bloc. The military took over in 1968, but civilian rule was restored in 1991. Multiparty elections took place in 1992.

Mauritania became independent in 1960, and a one-party state in 1965; a military government took control during the 1970s. In 1984 Maaouiya Ould Sidi Ahmed Taya seized power. In 1991 he restored multiparty democracy and was reelected in 1997.

Niger became independent from France in 1960. During the 1990s Tuareg rebels in the north fought for independence; a ceasefire was agreed in 1997. Multiparty rule, first introduced in 1991, and again in 1999, has been fragile.

Nigeria became independent in 1960. After conflict, such as the Biafran War (1967–1970), a series of military and often corrupt governments damaged the country. Civilian rule was restored in 1998, but problems remained, and ethnic conflict continued into 2002.

Senegal became independent in 1960 and has been politically stable. The first president set up a one-party, socialist state, but restored the country to multiparty democracy in 1974. Senegal formed a confederation with The Gambia, but it was dissolved in 1989.

Sierra Leone achieved independence in 1961. Since 1964 the country has been politically unstable. In 1978 it became a one-party state. Bitter civil war led to the arrival of UN peacekeeping forces in 1999 and, in 2002, the war was declared over.

Togo gained independence in 1960. Multiparty democracy was restored in 1991, but Gnassingbe Eyadéma continued to win presidential elections in 1993 and 1998, despite accusations of fraud.

CAPE VERDE
Praia
Nouadhibou
MAURITANI
Nouakchott
Sénégal
Kaédi
Dakar
SENEGAL
Thiès
Kayes
THE GAMBIA
Banjul
Gambia
Bissau
GUINEA-BISSAU
Labé
GUINEA
Kank
Conakry
SIERRA
Freetown
LEONE
Atlantic
Ocean
LIBER
Monrovia

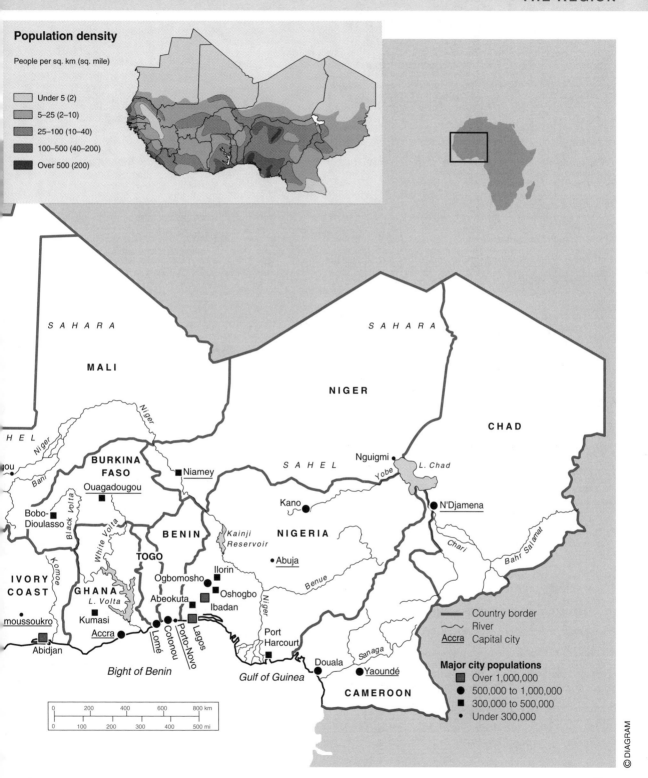

Population density

People per sq. km (sq. mile)

- Under 5 (2)
- 5–25 (2–10)
- 25–100 (10–40)
- 100–500 (40–200)
- Over 500 (200)

S A H A R A

MALI

S A H A R A

NIGER

CHAD

H E L

Niger

Niger

Bani

BURKINA
FASO

■ Niamey

Ouagadougou

S A H E L

Yobe

Nguigmi •

L. Chad

Kano ●

● N'Djamena

Bobo-
Dioulasso

Black Volta

White Volta

BENIN

Kainji
Reservoir

NIGERIA

Chari

Bahr Salamat

TOGO

• Abuja

Benue

IVORY
COAST

Komoe

GHANA

L. Volta

Ogbomosho

Ilorin ■

Niger

moussoukro

Kumasi ■

Abeokuta

Oshogbo

Ibadan

Accra ●

Lomé

Cotonou

Porto-Novo

Lagos

Port
Harcourt

Abidjan

Sanaga

Douala •

● Yaoundé

Bight of Benin

Gulf of Guinea

CAMEROON

Country border
River
Accra Capital city

Major city populations
- ■ Over 1,000,000
- ● 500,000 to 1,000,000
- ■ 300,000 to 500,000
- • Under 300,000

| 0 | 200 | 400 | 600 | 800 km |

| 0 | 100 | 200 | 300 | 400 | 500 mi |

© DIAGRAM

9

The languages of West Africa

There are many hundreds of ethnic groups in West Africa; in fact, there are more than 200 ethnic groups in Nigeria alone. As a result hundreds of languages are spoken in the region. Some languages, such as Dogon, spoken by the Dogon of central Mali, or Mande, the language of the Mende people of Sierra Leone, are specific to certain ethnic groups.

Other languages, however, are more widely spoken because of historical reasons. Arabic and Hausa languages were the language of trade and, nowadays, they are widely spoken by many groups. Muslims in West Africa learn Arabic because it is the language of the Qur'an, the holy book of Islam. English and French have also been spoken in the region since the colonial period.

It is difficult to classify African languages. More than 1,000 languages are spoken across the whole continent. Most are so-called home languages, which are native to Africa. Others were introduced by European or Asian colonizers. As a result, most Africans speak more than one language – their own ethnic language and a European language. Some West African languages also have dialects. The Ewe, Fon, and Fulfulde, the language of the Fulani, all have several dialects. Dyula is widely used as a common language and there are also Creole languages, such as Liberian Krio, which are a mix of African and European languages.

The colonial legacy

With the notable exception of Liberia, every country in West Africa was at some point colonized by European powers. As a result, European languages are spoken widely and, in some cases, they are the official languages of a country. English, French, and Portuguese are still widely spoken in West Africa because they were the languages of the major colonial powers who at one time had control over territories in the region.

Teaching the Qur'an
This wooden board is inscribed with a text from the Islamic holy book, the Qur'an. Such boards are used in schools to teach the Arabic language and the principles of Islam.

Professional storytellers
In West Africa such people are called *griots*; the one illustrated here attended the royal court, and was sketched by one of the first Europeans who visited the region in the colonial era.

African languages

The people of Africa speak more than 1,000 languages, most of them "home" languages native to the continent. The remaining languages, such as Arabic, English, or French, have all been introduced by settlers or invaders from Asia or Europe. The home languages are divided into four main families, within which are several subfamilies. These are then divided into groups and again into subgroups. Those languages spoken in West Africa are printed in *italic* type below.

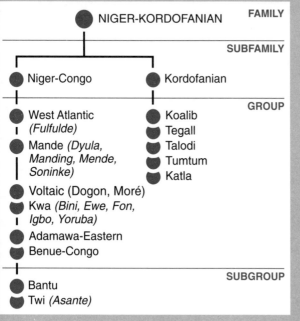

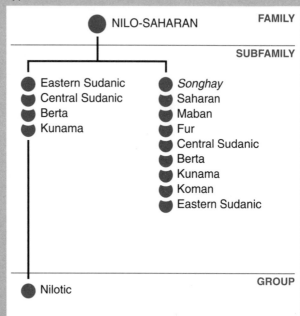

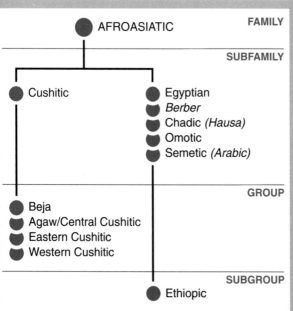

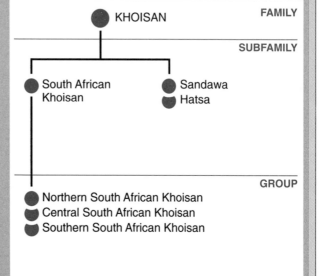

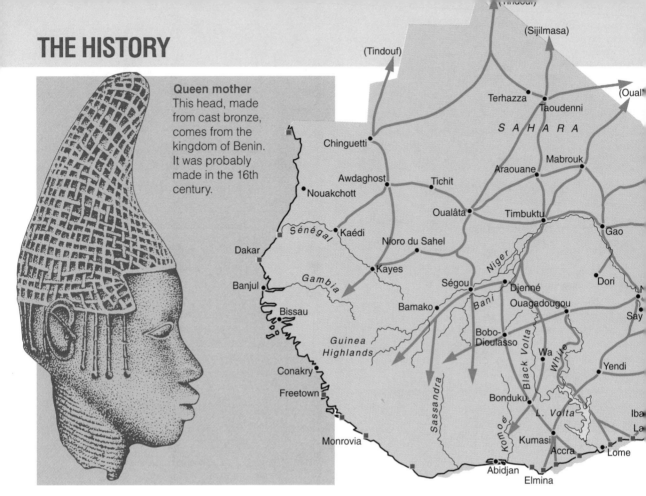

Queen mother
This head, made from cast bronze, comes from the kingdom of Benin. It was probably made in the 16th century.

The vast region of West Africa has an ancient history. Rock engravings and cave paintings in what is now Chad show that, some 5,000 years ago, early people were hunting and herding in the Sahara. By about 500 BCE, Bantu-speaking peoples emerged in what is now eastern Nigeria. They spread throughout West Africa and then made their way east and south throughout sub-Saharan Africa.

Great civilizations
West Africa was also the home of some of the continent's greatest civilizations. The earliest known was the Nok Culture which flourished in Nigeria from about 500 BCE to 200 CE. Other states emerged and, by the 15th century, four great civilizations or empires dominated the grasslands: ancient Ghana, Mali, Songhay and

Kanem-Borno. Other civilizations such as the Yoruba and Benin kingdom also appeared in the forests and coastal areas of West Africa.

Trade and slavery
Trade between West Africa and the peoples of North Africa goes back at least 2,000 years as traders and merchants crossed the great Sahara. From the 11th century, Muslim influence in West Africa has been significant. From the 16th century, West Africans developed trading links with Europeans who arrived on the coast. The Europeans came in search of gold and African slaves to work the plantations in their new American colonies. Slavery was not new to Africa and some kingdoms grew wealthy from the trade. Overall, however, the slave trade caused enormous suffering not only to Africans

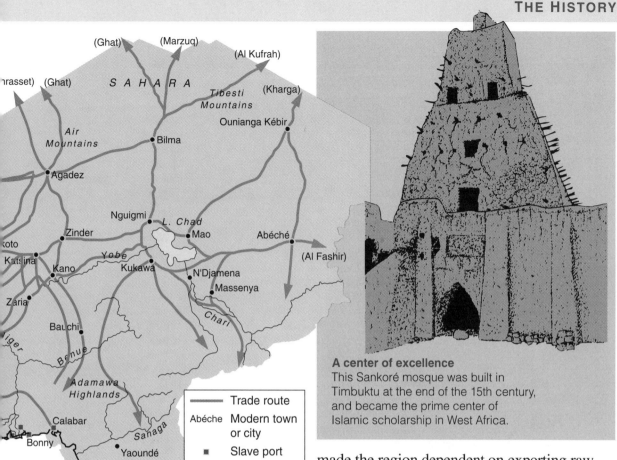

(Ghat) (Marzuq)
(Al Kufrah)

rasset) (Ghat) S A H A R A *Tibesti Mountains* (Kharga)

Air Mountains Bilma Ounianga Kébir

Agadez

Nguigmi *L. Chad* Mao Abéché

Zinder *Yobe* Kukawa (Al Fashir)

Koto Katsina Kano N'Djamena

Zaria Massenya

Bauchi *Chari*

Niger *Benue*

Adamawa Highlands

Calabar *Sanaga*

Bonny Yaoundé

Trade route	
Abéche	Modern town or city
◼	Slave port

A center of excellence
This Sankoré mosque was built in Timbuktu at the end of the 15th century, and became the prime center of Islamic scholarship in West Africa.

but also to the local societies and economies. By the time the slave trade ended in the 19th century, some 10 million Africans had been sold into slavery. Local African economies had been destroyed and wars and raids caused further hardship.

Colonialism and independence

Initially Europeans confined their influence to the coastal regions but, during the nineteenth century, explorers and colonizers moved farther inland. Despite fierce resistance, by 1914 all of West Africa, apart from Liberia, was under European colonial rule. The impact of colonialism on the region was enormous. It created the modern political boundaries and

made the region dependent on exporting raw materials rather than encouraging manufacturing. Nationalist movements emerged after World War II (1939–1945) and, by the 1970s, West Africa had achieved independence as 18 nations. However, the new nations had little relevance to earlier African states or ethnic groupings. As a result, the region has known considerable conflict since independence.

How we know

Information about West African history comes from many sources including archeological finds, written evidence from missionaries, explorers and settlers, and modern academics. Much history has also been passed down orally through the generations.

© DIAGRAM

Historical events

WEST AFRICAN EVENTS	WORLD EVENTS

c.5000 BCE TO 1000 CE

c.5000 BCE Rock paintings show herders in Sahara (Chad)	**510 BCE** Roman republic founded
500 Nok culture (Nigeria)	**c.30 CE** Jesus Christ crucified
c.1 CE Bantu-speaking peoples begin to leave the region	**c.300** Maya civilization emerges, Mexico
300 Ghana Empire emerges (Mali)	**622** Muhammad flees to Medina; Islam founded
c.700s Igbo Ukwu culture (Nigeria)	**624** T'ang dynasty unites China
c.750 Songhay state emerges (Mali)	
c.800 Kanem kingdom emerges (Lake Chad)	

1001 CE–1500 CE

1050 Islam introduced in West Africa	**c.1200** Inca Empire founded, Andes
c.1150 Ghana Empire reaches its height	**1206** Genghis Khan begins Mongol conquest, Asia
1200s Benin kingdom (Nigeria); Mossi states set up (Ghana)	**1300s–1402** Great Zimbabwe flourishes
1235 Mali Empire founded	**1346–1349** The Plague (Black Death) sweeps through Europe
c.1240 Mali absorbs Ghana and Songhay	**1368** Ming Dynasty, China
1300 Yoruba state, Oyo, created (Nigeria)	**1492** Christopher Columbus arrives in Americas
1443 Portuguese set up fort on coast (Mauritania)	
c.1490 Songhay Empire eclipses Mali	

1501–1800

1510 Atlantic slave trade begins	**1519–1522** Ferdinand Magellan sails around the world
c.1515 Songhay Empire reaches its height	**1521** Spain conquers Aztecs
1550 Wolof Empire ends; Mali collapses	**1526** Mughal Empire founded, India
1587 Portuguese seize Cape Verde Islands	**1590s** Dutch arrive at the Cape (South Africa)
1590 Moroccans defeat Songhay	**1619** First African slaves arrive at Jamestown, Virginia
1591 Kanem reaches greatest extent	**1657–1677** Dutch seize land from Khoikhoi (South Africa)
1625 Dahomey (Benin) founded	**c.1760** Industrial Revolution begins in Britain
1631 English set up first trading post on Gold Coast	**1776–1783** American Revolution
c.1640 Fante states develop (Ghana)	**1789–1799** French Revolution
1642 France founds trading post, Gambia River	
c.1650 Wadai Sultanate founded (Chad)	
1670s Asante clans unite (Ghana)	
1687 Portuguese found Bissau city as slave trade center	
1700 Kong kingdom emerges (Ivory Coast)	
1748 Oyo conquer Songhay	
1765 Britain creates colony of Senegambia	
1792 Freed Afro-American slaves settle what is now Freetown (Sierra Leone)	

1801–1850

1809 *Jihad* (holy war) defeats Fulani states. Fulani found Sokoto Caliphate (Nigeria)	**1816–1828** Chile, Venezuela, Brazil, Argentina, Peru, and Uruguay independent from Spain and Portugal
1816 Asante defeat Fante	**1821–1830** Greek War of Independence
1818 Dahomey breaks away from Oyo	**1846–1848** US-Mexican War
1824–1874 Anglo-Asante wars devastate Asante empire	**1848** *Communist Manifesto*
1836 Oyo disintegrates. Ibadan Empire emerges	
1847 Freed American slaves found Liberia	
1850s Wadai at greatest extent	

WEST AFRICAN EVENTS

WORLD EVENTS

1851–1900

1852	Tukolor empire (Mali)
1870s–1880s	Second Mandinka Empire set up (Senegal). It succeeds Mali Empire
1879	Rabib b. Fadl Allah begins to build empire (Chad/Nigeria)
c.1880	European "scramble" for Africa begins
1892	French conquer Dahomey
1893	Rabib defeats Kanem-Borno
1893	French defeat Tukolor Empire
1895	France creates federation of colonies, later French West Africa
1895	Mandinkas defeat Kong kingdom
1896	Asante becomes a British colony
1897	Britain conquers Benin kingdom and Ibadan Empire
1898	French conquer second Mandinka Empire

1861 Italy is unified
1868 Meiji restoration, Japan
1869 Suez Canal opens
1871 Unification of Germany
1884 Berlin Conference on Africa
1898 Spanish-American War
1899–1902 Anglo-Boer War

1901–1950

1901	French conquer Mossi states and Rabib's empire
1902	Asante annexed to Gold Coast (Ghana)
1903	Mauritania becomes French colony
1904	France annexes Dahomey (Benin)
1906	Slavery abolished in Gambia
1914	Europeans dominate all of West Africa apart from Liberia
1914–1918	World War I: West African troops fight on both sides
1922	Cameroon divided between France and Britain
1939–1945	World War II: West African troops fight on both sides
1948	Nationalist movement begins in French Cameroon

1904–1905 Russo-Japanese War
1905 First Russian Revolution
1914–1918 World War I
1917 Russian Revolution: Bolsheviks take power
1929 Wall Street Crash, US, leads to worldwide economic depression
1939–1945 World War II
1946 United Nations (UN) formed
1948 Apartheid introduced, South Africa
1949 Communists take power, China
1949 North Atlantic Treaty Organization (NATO) formed

1951–1970

1957	Gold Coast gains independence as Ghana, the first black African colony to achieve independence
1958–1975	All other West African nations achieve independence
1960–1972	Frequent military coups and government changes, Dahomey (Benin)
1963	Military coup, Togo
1963	Organization of African Unity (OAU) founded
1965	Civil war begins, Chad
1966	Military coup ousts Nkrumah, Ghana
1966	Guerilla activity begins, Chad
1966	Cameroon becomes one-party state
1967	Military coups: Sierra Leone, and Togo
1967–1970	Biafran War
1969–1970	Civilian rule returns: Ghana, Sierra Leone, Upper Volta

1950–1953 Korean War
1955 Warsaw Pact formed,
1959 Fidel Castro leads Cuban revolution
1962 Cuban missile crisis
1963 US president John F. Kennedy assassinated
1965–1973 US troops in Vietnam
1967 Six Day War between Israel and Egypt and other Arab nations
1969 Neil Armstrong lands on the Moon

© DIAGRAM

15

Colonial occupation and independence

WEST AFRICAN EVENTS

1971–1980

1972 Military coups: Dahomey and Ghana
1974 Military coups: Niger and Upper Volta
1974 Oil boom, Nigeria
1975 Dahomey is renamed Benin
1975 Military coup, Nigeria
1976 Economic Community of West African States (ECOWAS) is launched
1977 Nigeria hosts international Black Festival of Arts
1978 Civilian rule returns, Upper Volta
1978 Military coup: Mauritania
1979 Civilian rule returns, Benin and Nigeria
1980 Military coups: Liberia, Upper Volta, Guinea Bissau
1980 Libyan troops invade Chad

1981–2002

1981 Military coup led by Jerry Rawlings seizes power, Ghana
1982–1989 Senegal and Gambia united in Senegambia Confederation
1982 Oil production begins, Benin
1983 Military coups: Upper Volta and Nigeria
1984 Upper Volta is renamed Burkina Faso
1989 Civil war begins, Liberia
1990–2002 Intermittent civil war, Sierra Leone
1990–1997 Tuareg uprising, Niger
1990 Rebels overthrow government, Chad
1990 Multiparty elections held, Ivory Coast
1990 President Samuel Doe assassinated Liberia; civil war escalates
1991 Multiparty elections in Benin and Cape Verde
1991 Military rule ends, Burkina Faso
1992 Multiparty elections, Mali and Cameroon
1993 Ceasefire agreed, Liberia
1995 Military government in Nigeria executes nine Ogoni dissidents; Nigeria expelled from Commonwealth
1996 Military coup Nigeria
2000 UN peacekeeping troops in Sierra Leone
2001 Health crisis, Burkina Faso, following meningitis outbreak
2002 Civil war continues, Chad
2002 Ethnic and religious conflict continues, Nigeria
2002 Civil war breaks out in Ivory Coast and continues into 2003

WORLD EVENTS

1973 Arabs ban oil sales to US; sets off worldwide oil crisis
1973 Yom Kippur War between Egypt and Israel
1979 Islamic fundamentalists seize power in Iran
1979 Soviet Union invades Afghanistan
1980–1988 Iran-Iraq War

1982–1985 Israel invades Lebanon
1989 Revolution in Romania
1990 East and West Germany reunited
1990-1991 Gulf War follows Iraqi invasion of Kuwait
1991 Break up of Soviet Union; communism collapses in USSR and eastern Europe
1991 Apartheid ends, South Africa
1992 Cold War ends
1994–1996 Civil war, Rwanda; conflict spreads to Burundi
1998 Good Friday Agreement: peace in Northern Ireland
2001 Terrorist attack on World Trade Center, New York
2002 Israeli-Arab conflict escalates

COLONIAL OCCUPATION AND INDEPENDENCE

Country	Independence	Occupied*	Colonial powers
Benin (as Dahomey)	Aug 1, 1960	1892	France
Burkina Faso (as Upper Volta)	Aug 5, 1960	1892	France
Cameroon (as German Kamerun, French Cameroun, and British Cameroons)	Jan 1, 1960	1884	Germany 1884–1919; France and Britain divided and took control of Cameroon after Germany's defeat in WWI
Cape Verde	July 5, 1975	1587	Portugal
Chad (as part of French Equatorial Africa)	Aug 11, 1960	1900	France
Ivory Coast (as part of French West Africa)	Aug 7, 1960	1904	France
The Gambia	Feb 18, 1965	1816	Britain
Ghana (as Gold Coast)	March 6, 1957	1896	Britain
Guinea (as French Guinea)	Oct 2, 1958	1898	France
Guinea-Bissau (as Portuguese Guinea)	Sept 10, 1974	1880	Portugal
Liberia			Liberia has been independent since its establishment in 1847
Mali (as Soudan)	June 20, 1960	1898	France
Mauritania (as part of French West Africa)	Nov 28, 1960	1903	France
Niger (as part of French West Africa)	Aug 3, 1960	1908	France
Nigeria	Oct 1, 1960	1880	Britain
Senegal (as part of French West Africa)	June 20, 1960	1890	France
Sierra Leone	April 27, 1961	1787	Britain
Togo (as Togoland)	April 27, 1960	1884	Germany 1884–1919; France 1919–1960

*The years given for the beginning of colonial occupation of the modern-day nation states are those by which a significant area of coastal and hinterland territory had been effectively occupied by a colonial power.

THE STONE AGE

The human history of West Africa began millions of years ago – long before people knew how to use fire, farm crops, keep livestock, or work iron. Those times are known as the Stone Age because weapons and tools were mainly made from stone. The emergence of the first farmers and herders occurred toward the end of West Africa's Stone Age.

Archeologists are scientists who study the physical remains of early human life and activities. Such remains might include human fossils, artifacts, such as pots, stone tools, or ancient monuments. In East Africa archeologists found the remains of human ancestors more than 4 million years old, probably the oldest such remains in the world.

In West Africa, however, no such major finds of hominids (human ancestors) have been uncovered. This is partly because there have been relatively few archeologists working in the region, but also because the acidic tropical soils and hot, wet climate do not preserve bones or wood, which for a long time was a common building material in Africa, very well. Additionally, the fragile soil is easily eroded, that is carried away by wind or water. Much of the evidence of early human life in

'Toumaï'
This skull, which is believed to be between six and seven million years old, is the earliest known record of the family we now classify as human. It was found in the Djurabi desert of northern Chad. Pre-Stone Age, it may mark a significant stage in the development of chimpanzees into modern humans.

History of the Stone Age

2.5 mya	Early Stone Age begins. Hunter-gatherer societies emerge
100,000 BCE	Early Stone Age ends, and Middle Stone Age begins
60,000	Early humans are using fire in Africa
20,000	Sahara desert is at its driest
15,000	Middle Stone Age ends, and Late Stone Age begins. Microlith, or small stone, tool-making industries develop in some regions of West Africa
10,000	Sahara begins to become warmer, wetter, and greener than today
9000	People start to move into the Sahara desert. Elephants, hippos, and other animals inhabit the region
9000	Iwo Eleru occupied (present-day Nigeria)
6000	Cattle are kept in West Africa
4000–1000	Grain crops are farmed in West Africa
3000	Sahara begins to become drier again, and the desert expands. People living in the Sahara begin to move southward and northward
from 3000–2000	Yams and oil palms are farmed in forests
2000	Sahara desert reaches present-day extent
1000	Late Stone Age ends

West Africa, therefore, comes from long-lasting materials, such as stones and pieces of pottery.

In Africa, the Stone Age can be divided into three major periods: the Early Stone Age, which lasted from approximately 2.5 million years ago until 100,000 BCE; the Middle Stone Age, which lasted from around 100,000 BCE until 15,000 BCE; and, finally, the Late Stone Age, which lasted from around 15,000 BCE until 1000 BCE.

The Early Stone Age

During this period people had not yet evolved into modern humans; these early humans had smaller brains, and had only just begun to walk on two legs.

In West Africa, archeologists found evidence of these early hominids living on the Jos Plateau (modern Nigeria), the Futa Djallon highlands, and the lands north of the upper Sénégal River (in modern Senegal), and also in present-day Mauritania. The evidence found included simple stone tools, which were chipped together with other stones to produce sharp edges. These stone tools were then used to cut up dead animals.

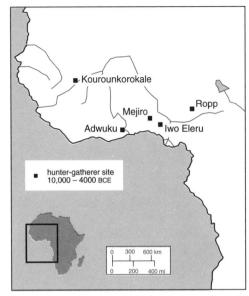

Stone-Age sites
Most Stone-Age sites, such as Iwo Eleru, date from the Late Stone Age; few artifacts of any historic significance have been found from earlier periods than this.

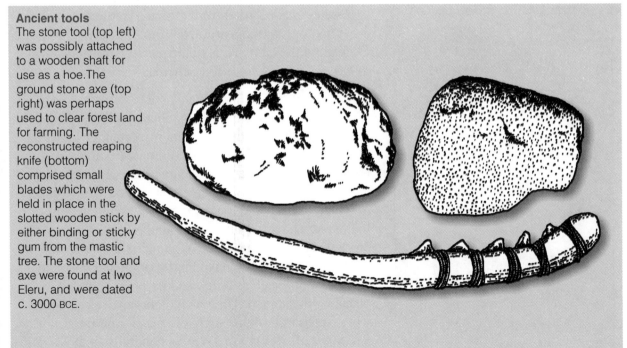

Ancient tools
The stone tool (top left) was possibly attached to a wooden shaft for use as a hoe.The ground stone axe (top right) was perhaps used to clear forest land for farming. The reconstructed reaping knife (bottom) comprised small blades which were held in place in the slotted wooden stick by either binding or sticky gum from the mastic tree. The stone tool and axe were found at Iwo Eleru, and were dated c. 3000 BCE.

© DIAGRAM

The development of the Stone Age

Fishing activity and pottery use in the late Stone Age, c.5000 BCE
The map (top) shows the area occupied by the Sahara today; it has fluctuated during the past 20,000 years owing to the climate changes that caused the Ice Ages farther north. The map (center) highlights the area of fishing activity (rivers. lakes, pools, and ponds); the remains of ancient fishing equipment have been found in lands now too dry to fish. The map (bottom) focuses on the area where pottery vessels were used by relatively settled people who spent much of the year in one place.

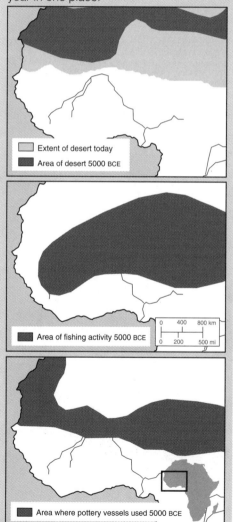

Extent of desert today
Area of desert 5000 BCE

Area of fishing activity 5000 BCE

0   400   800 km
0   200   500 mi

Area where pottery vessels used 5000 BCE

Early Stone Age people lived in small groups, probably moving from place to place in search of food. Plants were the most important source of food; people gathered fruits, seeds, nuts, and grubs from the wild to eat. They also prized wild animals for their meat, fur, skin, and even bones and teeth, which could be made into weapons. At first these animals were the remains of a predator's kill or the body of an animal that had died naturally. Hunting animals came later.

As hunting became more important, however, this may have led to a division of labor based on gender, with physically stronger and faster men doing the hunting, and women, who might have been nursing small children, doing the gathering. Even after the arrival of hunting, gathering still provided most of the group's food.

The Middle Stone Age
Hominids became very similar to modern humans during this period. They still found food much as their ancestors had by hunting and gathering. People made various stone tools dependent on the tasks they had to perform, and the types they made varied from region to region.

Archeologists found artifacts from this period on the Jos Plateau, in the Lirue Hills to the north of the plateau, and in Ghana, Ivory Coast, and Senegal.

The Late Stone Age
Modern humans were well-established in West Africa by this period, during which several important changes occurred. From 10,000 BCE the climate became drier, though not cooler, and the Sahara gradually expanded.

People learned how to make pottery and weave baskets in which to keep and transport goods, and they taught themselves how to build year-round homes. They also produced better stone tools; axes and other tools were no longer just chipped or flaked but ground and polished.

Small tools, such as arrow and harpoon heads, also became widespread. These and other small stone tools were called microliths. Archeologists found microliths at a number of sites in West Africa, generally in the savanna. Between the desert and the savanna lay the seasonally semiarid lands of the Sahel. There, people made harpoons and fish-hooks from bone but few microliths. In forested regions, people made ground-stone axes and pottery instead of microliths.

Climate change

Until 10,000 BCE, which marked the end of the last Ice Age, the Sahara was even drier than it is today. During the Ice Age, much of the Earth's water was frozen in huge glaciers to the north and south of Africa, with the result that rainfall there remained low.

As the glaciers melted, West Africa became increasingly wet and warm. Savanna, or tropical grassland, grew bigger at the expense of the Sahara and the forests in the south. People moved back into the desert, grasses flourished, and large animals, such as elephants, rhinos, hippos, and lions, lived in some places. This wet and warm period eventually came to an end, and the Sahara began to dry out again.

By 2000 BCE it reached its present-day extent.

Domestication

The most important development which eventually brought the Stone Age to a close was the domestication of plants and animals. Life as a hunter-gatherer was hard work, with members of a group spending much time looking for suitable items to gather or hunt.

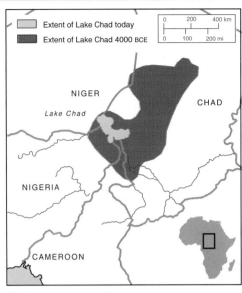

Prehistoric Lake Chad
Around 20,000 BCE Lake Chad disappeared completely because the region was much drier then. Between 10,000 BCE and 4000 BCE, the lake rose and fell in size several times, increasing its overall size each time. It reached its largest extent in 4000 BCE, but then shrunk as the region dried out.

Hunting hippos in the Sahara!
Late Stone Age Saharan people hunted hippos. At that time, hippos, crocodiles, and fish lived in the rivers that flowed across what is now the Sahara Desert. Ancient rock art, such as this example, reveals that the fishermen, who used harpoons and hooks, also knew how to build boats.

© DIAGRAM

The end of the Stone Age

Sub-Saharan rock art
The most characteristic sites in West Africa in which this form of art appeared were located south of the Sahara, somewhere between Senegal and Nigeria. The first mention of sub-Saharan art was published in 1907 by Louis Desplagnes following his survey of the central plateau of Niger. This particular illustration, which was found in a rock shelter, depicts a mission in what is now Mali, formerly the colony of French Sudan in French West Africa.

An elephant in rock
This several-thousand year-old rock painting depicts an elephant living in what is now the Sahara. Elephants, giraffes, and lions lived in the grasslands which, at that time, covered much of the present-day desert. As the climate changed, these animals either died out or migrated to more favorable regions.

A huge breakthrough was made when people realized that they could keep animals, and also have a ready supply of milk, leather, and meat. They learned that mating the best males and females increases the quality and amount of food the offspring provide. In Stone Age West Africa domesticated animals included cows, goats, and sheep. Around 100 BCE, the camel arrived, already domesticated, from North Africa.

A legacy of developments

Domesticating animals and plants allowed people to settle and develop larger and more complex societies. Because people could produce and store enough food to last at least a season, and survive such events as droughts, society grew more stable. People had more spare time to devote to tasks unrelated to food production, such as

pottery and basket making. These trends continued and
developed further during the Iron Age.

Domesticating animals (left)
This is an example of rock art from the
Sahara which shows people herding
cattle. After 6000 BCE, cattle appear more
and more frequently in Saharan rock art,
until they are almost commonplace. Other
rock art has revealed that people also
experimented, less successfully, with
domesticating other types of animals then
living in the Sahara, including giraffes.

© DIAGRAM

Early farming

When making pots, Stone Age people sometimes decorated them by pressing grains of millet, sorghum, or other crops into the unbaked clay. From these impressions, archeologists can determine the type of plants that existed thousands of years ago – the most important were millet and sorghum. It is difficult to know when crop farming first began in West Africa, but it was definitely sometime during the Late Stone Age.

Some historians believe farming was invented in West Africa independently from other parts of the world; others think it spread to West Africa from places such as Egypt and North Africa. Whichever is the case, West African farmers did farm their own food crops, because the staple grains (wheat and barley) of lands farther north are unable to thrive in the desert, savannas, or the tropics.

Instead, perhaps between 4000 and 1000 BCE, the first West African farmers turned to wild grasses that already grew in the region. People had been collecting the seeds of these grasses for a long time. Then, through trial and error, they learned how to sow them, and how best to tend the growing plants. From the wild seeds, people developed the millet grain crops, including sorghum (a type of millet), and pearl millet, a particularly hardy type.

Mande-speaking farmers in the upper river region of the Niger were probably the first to farm African rice. Oil palms, yams, and certain other vegetable crops, such as okra, were probably first domesticated by people living in regions not suitable for grain crops, in particular the lands between the forests of what are now modern-day Ghana and Nigeria.

Gourds, used hollow to make vessels called calabashes, have also been cultivated in West Africa from early times.

Oil palm
This variety of palm grows naturally along the edges of forests. West Africans have long used it for oil, food, building, and fishing materials. As people moved farther into the forests, they took with them the oil palm, and later the yam.

Millet (left) and guinea corn (right)
These two cereal crops withstand drought well and require little rainfall in order to grow; they are mostly used in the preparation of porridge, flatbreads or cakes, and also the brewing of beer.

Okra
This vegetable (which is also known as gumbo) is native to West Africa. Its pods are used to thicken soups and stews.

Yam (top) and cocoyam (bottom)
The yam is a large tuber, the flesh and leaves of which are prepared in a similar way to cassava. Although similar in use and appearance to yams, cocoyams (or *taro* or *dasheen*) are considered much tastier.

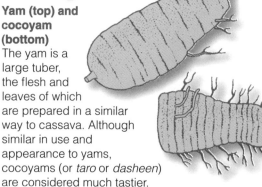

Domestication of rice and millet

African rice developed from a wild grass that grew in water holes. The holes filled up in the wet season but dried out in the dry season, making the rice particularly hardy. Today, it has largely been replaced by Asian varieties. There are several different strains of millet. Pearl millet originated from the present-day Senegal-Mauritania region.

Domestication of guinea corn (sorghum) and yams

Yams, like oil palms, were probably first cultivated on the margins of forests, around 4,000 to 5,000 years ago. Guinea corn is native to West Africa, and probably spread from there to other parts of the world; it is now grown in Asia and the Americas.

Introduction of crops from abroad

Hausa potatoes, and groundnuts (or peanuts) are nowadays very important crops in West Africa. They are not native to the region, however, but were probably introduced by Portuguese sailors in the 1400s. However, strains of these crops were grown and domesticated (bred) in this region, and some experts believe that one type of groundnut could even be native to West Africa.

© DIAGRAM

THE IRON AGE

West Africa's Iron Age began more than 2,500 years ago. People learned how to work iron, and this brought huge social change. Some of the oldest cities and civilizations of Africa south of the Sahara emerged in Iron Age West Africa. One of these, the Nok Culture, produced some of the continent's finest art ever.

In the 20th century, a tin miner working on central Nigeria's Jos Plateau near the village of Nok made a startling discovery – he unearthed the first of several fine pottery heads. Made from baked clay, the heads were produced by an iron-working people. When archeologists investigated further they discovered iron-smelting furnaces that were at least 2,500 years old. They remain the oldest-known iron-working sites in West Africa.

Shaping metal
Two men make spears in the traditional way. Africans were also skilled in fashioning barbs, lances, ceremonial axes, and throwing knives.

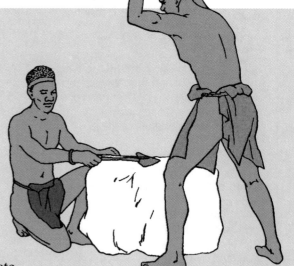

Metalworking

Iron is a hard metal, but the rocks that contain it are relatively common, more so than those that contain copper or tin. Copper and tin, however, are softer and easier to work. In most parts of the world, people used copper or tin before they worked iron. In the Middle East around 3,500 years ago, people learned how to heat copper ore (metal-containing rocks) to separate the metal from the rocks. This is called smelting. Next, people learned that copper mixed with tin produced bronze (an alloy, or mixture); bronze is harder than copper alone. Iron is even harder again, but it is more difficult to produce. To separate iron from its ore, the rocks need to be heated to great temperatures.

It took a while to develop the technology that could do this: furnaces that both inject air into the fire to raise the temperature, and use charcoal to lower the rock's melting point. The iron could then be hammered into shape by blacksmiths. West Africans used iron to make weapons such as spearheads and axes, tools, and jewelry such as bracelets.

Spread and origins of iron working

In West Africa, metalworking probably followed the same pattern of development – copper and tin being worked first, then bronze, then iron – but only limited evidence of early copper or tin working has been found in the region. The first metal some people smelted may have been iron. This suggests that iron-working was introduced into the region from elsewhere (because historians assume that iron-working skills can only be invented by people who already know how to work the softer metals copper or tin). In that case, iron-working skills probably spread to West Africa from the Middle East via North Africa or from Ancient Egypt via East Africa.

Some historians think, however, that iron-working was invented independently in West Africa, and spread through the region at a relatively slow pace. Archeologists have found evidence of people working iron more than 2,000 years ago in burial mounds in the Niger Valley and southwest Chad, as well as around the village of Nok. In northern Sierra Leone, however, the earliest evidence dates from the 700s CE. In the forested regions, iron was worked by the end of the first millennium CE, at such sites as Igbo Ukwu.

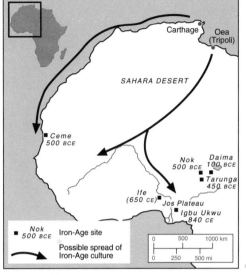

Iron-working
This map shows the location of Iron-Age sites in the region of West Africa. The dates, when shown in brackets, are accurate within one century. Arrows indicate the possible spread of iron-working culture, together with approximate dates.

Standing stones
These ancient stones stand in a field in The Gambia. Who made them, or what they were used for is not known, but it is believed they were associated with burials. They date from the second half of the first millennium CE.

The development of the Iron Age

Nok sculpture
This head dates from between 500 BCE and 200 CE. Known as the Dinya (or D'jena) head, it was found by a tin miner near the village of Nok. This life-size head was probably once part of a complete figure.

Nearly 3,000 years ago, the Nok Culture emerged in what is now central Nigeria, on the Jos Plateau. It is West Africa's oldest known civilization, and also the site of the region's first ironworks. Nok smelters used furnaces with low shafts, perhaps with bellows, which blow air into the fire, thus raising its temperature. The furnaces had a depression at their base for removing slag (molten waste).

Historians do not know much about the Nok Culture, but it existed from about 900 BCE to 200 CE. The civilization has become famous for the beautiful terracotta (baked clay) figurines associated with it including, in particular, many finely crafted pottery heads. Since the first discovery of these near the village of Nok, terracotta figurines have been found over a much wider area in Nigeria. As well as being from the earliest sites of ironworking in West Africa, these artworks are the first examples of a developed sculptural tradition in Africa south of the Sahara.

The more recent sculptural traditions of Ife and Benin, which also produced magnificent artworks, could have developed out of the Nok Culture's tradition.

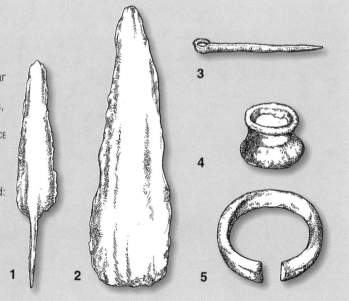

Mdaga artifacts
Mdaga was a burial mound in southwest Chad that was 980 ft (300 m) long, 600 ft (185 m) wide, and 26 ft (8 m) high. The oldest parts dated from c.150 BCE. Humar skeletons, ceramics, terracotta statues, animal bones, stone tools, as well as iron and copper items and iron slag dating from c.100 BCE (the earliest evidence of iron use), were found on the mound. The following illustrations offer some idea of the craftsmanship involved:
1 Iron spearhead
2 Iron ax
3 Iron spindle
4 Lip plug in alloyed copper
5 Alloyed copper bracelet

Iron Age societies

Once people learned how to smelt iron, they were able to make better tools, farm more crops, and make stronger weapons. Before this, weapons and tools were made from wood or stone. Eventually, as farming techniques continued to improve, people found they produced more food than they needed or could store. These surpluses could be traded, so trade and business developed, and people increasingly found ways other than farming to make their living. Some worked as traders, tailors, soldiers, or religious and political officials. Iron-working communities included miners, smelters, and blacksmiths.

Urbanization

This growth of trade and activities other than farming allowed population levels to increase. Eventually, the first urban areas emerged. To be urban, an area must be occupied largely by people who do not make their living from the land. One of the first cities south of the Sahara was Jenne-jeno on the Niger River in what is now Mali. The island was settled by iron-workers by 250 BCE.

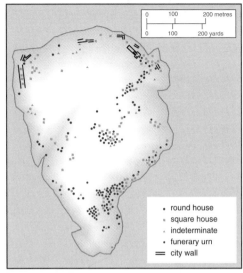

- • round house
- ▪ square house
- · indeterminate
- · funerary urn
- = city wall

Plan of a city
Jenne-jeno was enclosed by a city wall which was 1.25 miles (2 km) long and 36 ft (11 m) wide. It contained both round and square mud-brick houses, and a certain number of structures of indeterminate shape. Burial urns were located around both the residential area and the cemetery.

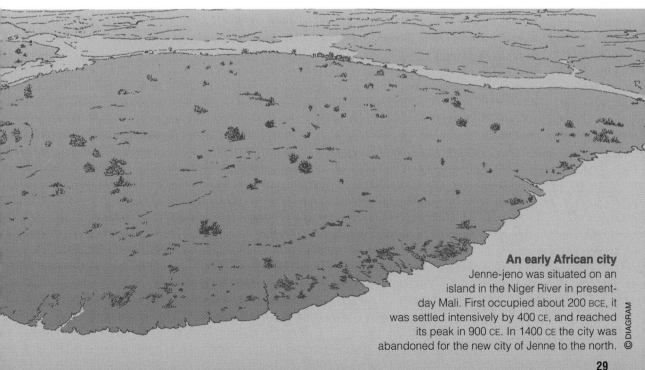

An early African city
Jenne-jeno was situated on an island in the Niger River in present-day Mali. First occupied about 200 BCE, it was settled intensively by 400 CE, and reached its peak in 900 CE. In 1400 CE the city was abandoned for the new city of Jenne to the north.

© DIAGRAM

The Igbo-Ukwu culture

More than 1,200 years ago, the Igbo Ukwu culture flourished in what is now southeast Nigeria. It probably existed as early as the ninth century CE.

The first evidence of this civilization was unearthed by accident, in a similar way to that of the discovery of the Nok Culture. A man was digging up earth to build a house when he found the first of many beautiful terra cotta and bronze objects for which Igbo Ukwu has since become famous. The bronzes are the oldest metal sculptures that have yet been found in West Africa.

Trading state

Historians once thought that people living in, and around, the forests of West Africa were not part of any long-distance trade networks until Europeans came to the coast from the 1400s onward. Evidence from Igbo Ukwu, and elsewhere, has disproved this. Grave goods included raw materials, such as semiprecious carnelian stones and copper, that were not common in the nearby lands. Some might have come from as far away as India or Persia (modern-day Iran).

The most plentiful copper mines in West Africa at that time were far to the north at Takedda (modern Niger) in the Sahara. Takedda supplied Igbo Ukwu with copper, and linked it with the trans-Saharan trade routes.

Feathered fan
This copper fan-holder was found in the burial chamber of a dignitary at Igbo Ukwu. Feathers have been added around the crescent to show how it would probably have looked when the culture was at its height around the ninth century CE.

Trade goods

Metal tools were made for local use, or to trade with people on the coast and farther inland. Like other Niger delta communities, the people of Igbo Ukwu sent salt and dried fish north in exchange for agricultural produce; other goods were traded to the east and west.

Igbo kings

One Igbo proverb says: "The Igbo have no kings."

While this is true more recently, grave goods found at Igbo Ukwu suggest that the Igbo, or at least certain Igbo peoples, do have a tradition of kingship.

One pit associated with the priest-king's grave contained around 165,000 glass and stone beads, as well as more than 680 copper and bronze items. For one individual to amass such wealth, a powerful central authority probably existed.

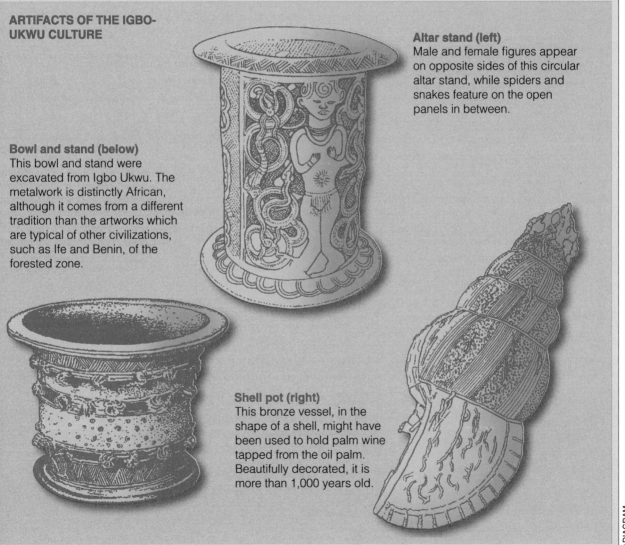

ARTIFACTS OF THE IGBO-UKWU CULTURE

Altar stand (left)
Male and female figures appear on opposite sides of this circular altar stand, while spiders and snakes feature on the open panels in between.

Bowl and stand (below)
This bowl and stand were excavated from Igbo Ukwu. The metalwork is distinctly African, although it comes from a different tradition than the artworks which are typical of other civilizations, such as Ife and Benin, of the forested zone.

Shell pot (right)
This bronze vessel, in the shape of a shell, might have been used to hold palm wine tapped from the oil palm. Beautifully decorated, it is more than 1,000 years old.

© DIAGRAM

GHANA AND ITS NEIGHBORS

The Soninke people live in present-day Mali, Burkina Faso, Senegal, and Mauritania. More than 1,000 years ago they founded the first well-organized and well-armed civilization in Africa south of the Sahara. It was called ancient Ghana.

Soninke tradition, as retold in 16th-century chronicles, holds that this kingdom – called Ghana – was founded in the fourth century CE. However, the first hard evidence of the state's existence comes from the eighth century. The Soninke founders called their kingdom Wagadu but, to others, it came to be known by the title of its ruler, the *ghana. Gana,* or *kana,* means king or war chief. The ancient empire of Ghana is not related to the modern-day state of the same name, which lies farther south.

Growth and decline

By the ninth century, Ghana was a powerful centralized kingdom. By the end of the tenth century, the king of Ghana also had authority over neighboring smaller kingdoms; kings of these vassal states attended the *ghana*'s court freely or were held hostage there. To retain daily control of their kingdoms, they had to pay taxes to the *ghana* and obey his commands.

At its height, in the mid-11th century, Ghana's king ruled over what are now central Mali, eastern Senegal and Gambia, and southern Mauritania. Then, Ghana had a 200,000-strong army, of whom around 40,000 were archers, and it also had a large cavalry contingent.

Ghana lost the important Saharan trading town of Awdaghost to the Almoravids in 1054. The Almoravids, from North Africa, grew increasingly powerful in the region as they attempted to gain control over profitable trade routes. In 1076, the Almoravids conquered Ghana. They kept control for only a decade or so, and Ghana remained powerful for many more decades.

c.1000

Legend	
■ Empire of Ghana	□ Kingdom of Songhay
□ Kingdom of Kangaba (later Mali)	⬭ Gold field

Niger · Falémé · Bakoye · Niger · Kangaba

0 150 300 km
0 100 200 mi

Empire of Ghana, c. 1000 CE
This map shows Ancient Ghana 50 years before it reached its greatest extent; it went on to conquer the kingdoms of Songhay and Kangaba. The Bambuk and Bure goldfields lay south of the empire.

A victim of its own success

To support Ghana's large population, plentiful resources of water, soil, and timber were needed. Wealth from trade allowed these needs to be met to a certain extent, but Ghana lost control of trade centers to the north.

Once the Almoravids moved on, desert traders competed to control the trade routes, and invested their wealth in increasingly large herds of cattle. Pasture was in short supply in this dry region, and many lands became so overgrazed they turned into desert. Ghana's northern and central lands were lost to the desert and cities, including Awdaghost, were abandoned.

In an attempt to regain control of the trade routes, the most profitable of which now skirted Ghana to the east, the capital city might have been moved south, but whether this is correct or not is not known for sure.

The power of people to the south increased as that of Ghana diminished. They lived in more fertile lands nearer to the goldfields and the Niger River, which was used for transportation.

In the 13th century, rebellions and invasions by the southerly Susu people weakened Ghana. The Susu were, in turn, conquered by the founders of the Mali Empire. In 1240, the capital city of Ghana was destroyed by troops of the Mali emperor, and what remained became part of Mali.

An Arab trader

Much of the information about the empire of Ghana and other early West African states was provided by Arab geographers and historians who followed trade routes, and traders, around Africa. The introduction of the camel to Africa, c.100 CE, enabled more goods to be moved across the desert faster, thus increasing long-distance trade.

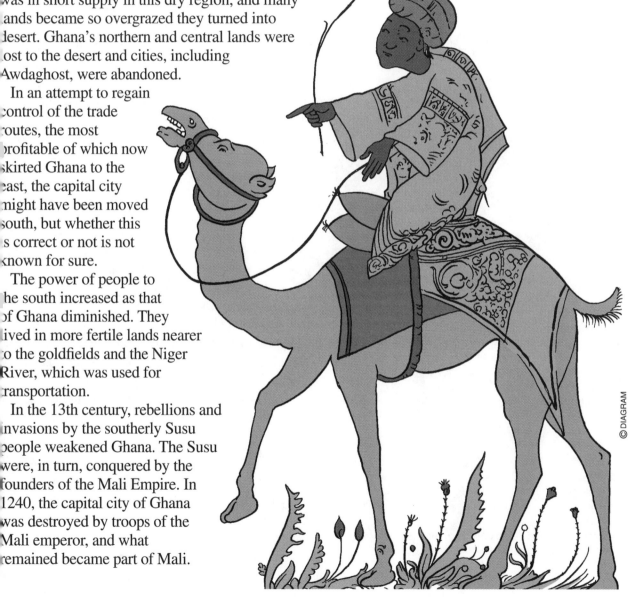

©DIAGRAM

Ghana – the "land of gold"

Camel caravan
A small caravan crosses the Sahara. Caravans could be much larger than this, often with several hundred animals. Traders preferred to travel in groups for protection as well as for economic reasons.

Human snake
Ancient Ghanaians worshiped spirit serpents, such as Ouagadou-Bida. This pottery fragment is of a human-snake head.

Arab coins
These Arab gold coins date from the 12th and 13th centuries. West Africa was an important source of gold for Arabia, then Europe, and eventually the whole world.

Ghana was perfectly positioned, between goldfields to the south, and near the ends of desert trade routes to the north, to benefit from the trans-Saharan trade in gold. Ghana grew rich on the trade in this gold; in fact early travelers called the empire the "land of gold." The precious metal was collected from people located at the goldfields of Bambuk and Bure to the south, and traded with people farther north for salt and other goods. At times salt was as valuable as gold. A wealthy class of merchant traders emerged. They paid taxes and tolls to the state. At times, people were only allowed to trade in gold dust. Nuggets of gold were kept by the king; this was to stop gold becoming too common and decreasing in value.

The more wealth Ghana collected, the bigger the army the state was able to maintain. With this army, Ghana extended its frontiers. Some nations allied themselves with the empire willingly, so that they, too, could benefit from the lucrative trade Ghana dominated. Important trading centers flourished around the empire, including Awdaghost, which was situated just north of it. In the 10th century, Arab merchant Ibn Hawqal reported seeing a check from an Awdaghost trader for 40,000 dinars (100,000 silver dollars) – a fortune in any era but especially so more than 1,000 years ago.

Neighbors

Was Ghana the first well-organized, militarily capable civilization in West Africa, as many historians think? Or was it simply the first of which we know? Ghana's position between the forests and the desert made it more accessible to travelers from the north than states farther south. Al Bakri, an Arab geographer, reported, however, that kingdoms called Malal and Daw existed to the south

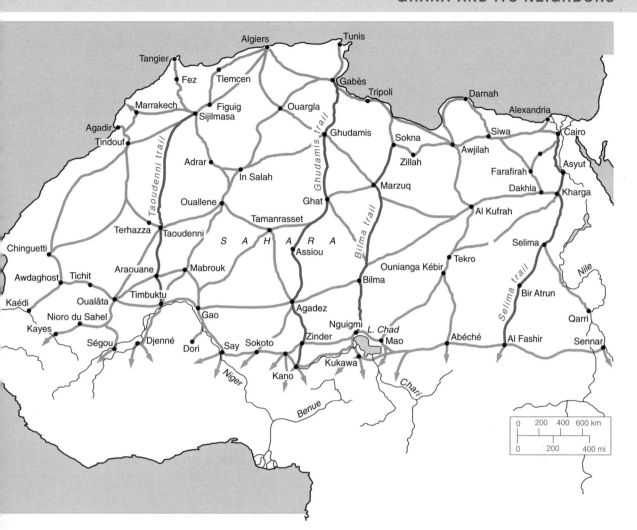

Trans-Saharan trade routes

of Ghana, but he never ventured that far south so little beyond the names he gave them are known.

Without doubt, Ghana was not the only civilization to emerge in West Africa in the first millennium. The kingdom of Kangaba existed farther south by 750 CE. Nearly 500 years later, Kangaba became the Mali Empire. Southwest of Ghana lay Takrur, in the valley of the Sénégal River, which existed from the 11th century. It is credited with being the first Muslim state in West Africa, though its rulers probably converted only a few decades before those of Ghana. To the east of Ghana, Kanem Bornu was founded in the ninth or 10th centuries.

Trans-Saharan trade routes
A network of trade routes has long crossed the Sahara. Although many have now been abandoned, some are still in regular use today. Ghana controlled the southern ends of the trade routes in West Africa, and collected gold from people to the south of the empire. Salt, dates, cloth, copper beads, weapons, and books were traded along the routes from north to south. Gold, ivory, ostrich feathers, leather, kola nuts, shells, beads, and slaves were traded along the routes from south to north. Ideas, religions, and languages also made the journey across the Sahara.

Ghana – a center of culture

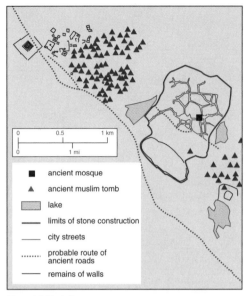

Kumbi Saleh

This was almost certainly the capital of the ancient empire of Ghana. The plan (above) shows a mosque at the centre of the Islamic part of the city. The illustration (below) represents a stone construction which was recently excavated. The non-Islamic part, where the king lived, has yet to be found.

Arab geographer Al Bakri reported in the 1060s that the *ghana* ruled his subjects indirectly through a network of ministers of state. Officials were often Muslims who could keep records in Arabic, and who made for better links with the trans-Saharan traders. Al Bakri described the king as autocratic – he ruled with unlimited power and answered to no one – but also as a lover of justice. The king inherited his title not from his father but from his mother, who was the sister of the king. This type of inheritance is called matrilineal descent.

Culture and religion

The kings of Ghana were considered to be divine. They were the focus of a religion practiced by priests near the capital. People believed that the wellbeing of the nation and its citizens was directly linked to the health and fortunes of its king. After a king's death, the *ghana* was buried under a great mound made of earth and supported by timber. Servants were killed and buried with him.

The arrival of Islam

Trade with Muslim Arabs from the north brought all the kingdoms on the southern fringes of the Sahara in touch

with Muslims. After the Almoravid invasion, the ruling classes and merchants of Ghana converted to Islam. The royal religious cult surrounding the king survived the introduction of Islam, however, even after the king, too, converted. Most of Ghana's citizens still followed their own religion, but the ruling classes and the king adopted Islam.

The king did not, however, forsake the original religion of Ghana. The kings of Ghana were wise enough to realize that their empire would benefit if they practiced both the religion of the trans-Saharan traders (Islam) as well as the religion of their people.

City life

The capital city, Kumbi Saleh, became a center of Islamic learning. It developed into two parts: an Islamic city and a non-Islamic city. The king lived in the older, pre-Islamic, city in a palace surrounded by a stone wall. The houses in the king's city were made from earth while those in the Islamic section were constructed out of stone.

Epic poetry

Heroic stories on a grand scale, epic poetry often relates the deeds of legendary characters, or the histories of important states. The Soninke founders of Ghana created the *Dausi*, epic poems that related the part-legendary, part-true story of Wagadu, their name for the Ghana empire. Often sung by *griots,* or storytellers, at gatherings and special occasions, epic poems were a way of passing history from one generation to the next.

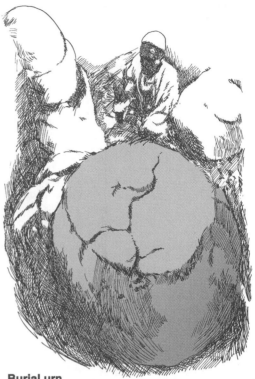

Burial urn
This burial urn from Jenne-jeno in central Mali contained a whole body. People were buried in urns from 450 to 1300 CE, which indicates that indigenous African religions remained important even as Islam spread through the region of West Africa.

Mound burial
The kings of ancient Ghana were buried in mounds like this one at El Oualedji, Mali.

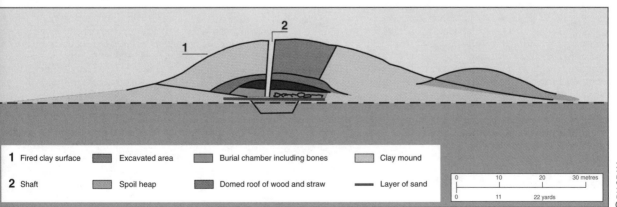

1 Fired clay surface	Excavated area	Burial chamber including bones	Clay mound
2 Shaft	Spoil heap	Domed roof of wood and straw	Layer of sand

| 0 | 10 | 20 | 30 metres |
| 0 | 11 | 22 yards | |

© DIAGRAM

MALI AND ITS NEIGHBORS

The Mali Empire was founded in the 1200s and grew to become one of the largest empires in the world at that time. Mali, through its traders, wealth, and the spread of Islam, had a great impact on the whole of West Africa.

As the Ghana empire declined, Mande-speaking people from the south struggled to take over its legacy. At first, early in the 1200s, the Susu, led by Sumunguru, proved the most successful. They were soon challenged by Malinke-speaking Mande people, who had founded the Kangaba kingdom in 750.

"Lion of Mali"

In 1234 the Susu overran Kangaba. The invaders put to death all the royals except for one crippled prince, Sundiata. One year later he defeated the Susu and, by 1240, he had conquered what was left of Ghana, and the empire of Mali came into existence. Mali means the "place where the king (*ma*) lives" in Malinke, and Sundiata came to be known as the "Lion of Mali."

Growth and decline

South of Segu on the Niger, the Songhay people controlled the transportation of goods along the great river. By conquering the Songhay, in the late 1200s, Mali was able to extend its lands to the east and south, absorbing many non-Mande peoples. By the 1300s, Mali had grown to be even more powerful than Ghana.

Under its most powerful *mansa* (king), Musa (reigned 1312–1337), the empire reached its greatest extent. It stretched from the Atlantic Ocean in the west more than

Kora players

These musicians are playing a stringed instrument called a *kora.* Sundiata, the founder of the Mali Empire, is credited with inventing this West African instrument, which is now most common in modern-day Gambia and Senegal. The *kora* often accompanies *griots,* or storytellers, as they sing songs that relate the history of ancient Mali.

1,250 miles (2,000 km) to the borders of modern Nigeria n the east, and from the southern edge of the Sahara to he borders of the forests 600 miles (965 km) to the south. This included most of modern Mali but also present-day Senegal, Gambia, Guinea Bissau, parts of Mauritania, and even southern Algeria.

Ancient Mali controlled not only the southern ends of he trans-Saharan trade routes but also the goldfields of Bambuk and Bure farther to the south. More gold came from the forest-living Akan peoples to the south, who traded much of their gold with Mali.

c.1300

Senegal
Niger
Gambia
Kangaba
Black
White
Volta
Atlantic Ocean

| 0 | 300 | 600 km |
| 0 | 200 | 400 mi |

Kingdom of Kangaba c.1235
Empire of Mali c.1300
Takrur c.1300
Gold field

Mali, Kangaba, and Takrur, c.1300

This map shows Mali as well as the small kingdom of Kangaba from which it emerged. Takrur, which was probably the first Muslim state in West Africa, lies to the east.

A typical Malinke town

The Malinke inhabitants of Kangaba, and Mali lived in round adobe houses, and stored their grain in barrel-like structures (visible in center).

© DIAGRAM

Mali – a trading empire

Great mosque
The Great Mosque of Jenne has stood on the same site since its foundation in the 1200s. The adobe structure has been rebuilt or repaired on a number of occasions.

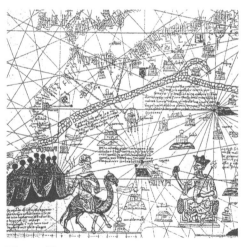

Mansa Musa
The emperor of Mali can be seen on this map holding up a nugget of gold to trade with the Arab merchant riding toward him on a camel. This is from the first European map of West Africa, drawn in 1375. Mali's fame had spread far by the 14th century. Much of Europe's gold came from West Africa, via the trans-Saharan trade.

In 1324 *Mansa* Musa set off on a pilgrimage to Mecca, the holy city of Islam, in Arabia. For centuries afterward, Arab historians wrote of Musa's impressive entourage. He traveled with thousands of finely dressed attendants and courtiers, and huge amounts of gold and jewelry. They spent so much gold when passing through Cairo, Egypt, that its value was significantly lowered.

Decline

After Musa's death, there was a dispute over who should succeed him. Although his brother, Suleiman, eventually inherited the throne, similar disputes in the Mande heartland weakened the empire as a whole. Although Mali survived until 1550, when it was conquered by Songhay, it was no longer politically important in the region by 1490.

Trade

Mali traded gold, ivory, ostrich feathers, leather, grain, and slaves for kola nuts, cowrie shells, copper beads, semiprecious stones, horses, and salt with traders from across the Sahara. Salt came both from the coast, where it was extracted from seawater, as well as from deposits in the desert. Marble gravestones inscribed with Arabic script found near Gao on the Niger River provide impressive evidence of this long-distance trade. The stones were probably made to order in Spain and transported across the Sahara in the 12th or 13th centuries. The empire benefited from this trade through tolls and taxes. Tribute was paid to the emperor by conquered nations.

The traders (literally *dyula*) of Mali emerged as a separate class, and they spread widely throughout West Africa, establishing urban areas and spreading Islam. Traders from Mali introduced Islam to the Hausa states of what is now northern Nigeria. Such merchants are the origin of the modern-day Dyula (or Jola) people, who mostly live in southern Senegal and Gambia, but whose language is widely spoken throughout West Africa by regional traders today.

Ways of life

The majority of people made their living by farming the land and/or keeping animals. The fertile floodplains of the inland Niger Delta, and to the south of Lake Chad, were particularly good for farming. As the yearly flood waters retreated, they left silt that enriched the soil. It was in such areas that the first cities and towns emerged, probably because the people were able to produce a surplus of food to trade. People also hunted wild animals and fished the rivers.

However, life was not easy for a great part of the time. The life-giving rivers were also linked to many serious diseases, including malaria, river blindness, and sleeping sickness. Many made their living solely through trade, especially in the cities and towns. Others were soldiers; Mali maintained an army of 100,000 soldiers and a cavalry of around 10,000 mounted troops.

Royal slaves

Each year the *mansa*'s cavalry ventured into the countryside of the inland Niger River. They captured healthy men who were either traded as slaves, or settled in colonies on the river. These slave colonies were visited each year by boats that collected the grain produced; it was then either traded or used to feed the royal court.

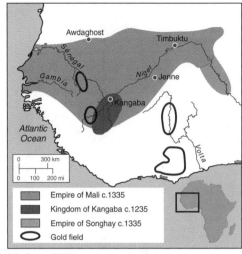

Mali, c. 1335
Mali was at its greatest extent, and one of the greatest empires in the world, under the control of *Mansa* Musa. Gao, Timbuktu, and Awdaghost were important urban centers at the ends of trans-Saharan trade routes.

Fired-clay statue
This beautiful terracotta statue was found in the Jenne region of central Mali. It was made sometime between 1000 and 1600. Many small statues dating from this time have been found in this particular region of Mali.

Mali – a safe environment

Malian gold coin
There are many burial mounds in West Africa. This beautifully decorated gold disk was part of the grave goods found in such a mound in Rao in northwest Senegal. Dating from the time of ancient Mali, which was probably the 13th or 14th century, the coin measures more than 7 inches (175 mm) in diameter, and was worn as jewelry.

Mansa Musa made Mali a unified and strong land with one system of law and order. In the Mande heartland, the basic political unit was the *kafu,* a community of one or several thousand people living in or near a walled town ruled by a *fama.* The position of *fama* was inherited.

Deputies, who were often members of the royal family, ruled conquered lands on behalf of the king. Or, members of the conquered royal families were held hostage at the *mansa*'s court to ensure obedience to Mali. Musa had ambassadors in Morocco, Egypt, and elsewhere.

Even after his death, the empire remained a safe and peaceful place in which to live. Moroccan Ibn Battuta traveled around Mali in the 1300s, and commented that the ordinary people were:

". . . seldom unjust, and have a greater abhorrence of injustice than any other people. Their sultan shows no mercy to anyone guilty of the least act of it. There is complete security in their country. Neither traveler nor inhabitant has anything to fear from robbers or men of violence."

A cultural legacy
Founded more than 2,250 years ago, Jenne-jeno developed into the important urban area of Jenne within the empire of Mali. Pottery, made between 850 and 1400, bears witness to the artistry and skill of the people who lived in the original town.
1 Fragment of the rim of a pot
2 Rim fragment imprinted with a bird's image
3 Fragment of the lid of a pot

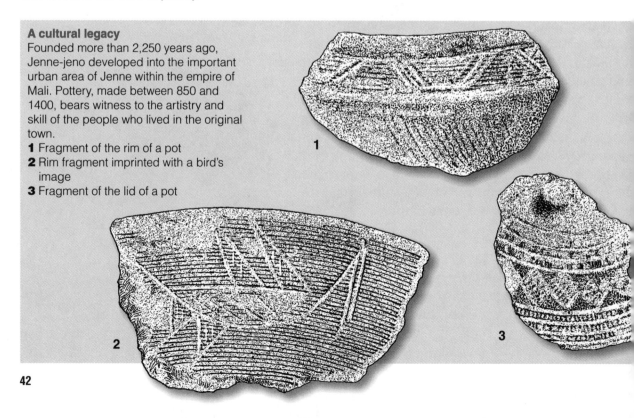

Town life

By the time of Mali, there had been towns, such as Jenne-eno, on the floodplains of the Niger and Sénégal rivers for centuries. Jenne, about 2 miles (3 km) west of Jenne-eno, developed at the expense of the latter, which began to shrink in the 1200s, and was finally abandoned in the 1400s. Some historians think Niana, farther south on the Niger River, was the capital of Mali. It was definitely an urban center of great importance, and was first settled several centuries before Mali came into existence. All these towns were cultural melting pots inhabited by people who spoke many different languages, from both West and North Africa.

The spread of Islam

Belief in Islam became increasingly important during the flourishing of the Mali Empire. With its great size and extensive trading networks, Mali helped spread the faith widely in West Africa.

During *Mansa* Musa's reign, Islam was still largely the religion of the ruling and trading classes, but these people made up a significant and influential proportion of the population. Like Mali's and Ghana's kings before him, Musa was a Muslim, although most of his citizens were not. In fact he still supported the Mande religion, with its various spirits and gods. These gods were often associated with particular aspects of Mande life, such as farming or fishing. People of many different religions and customs were allowed at Musa's court.

Musa and other kings helped establish the traditions of Islamic scholarship and building at cities, such as Jenne and Timbuktu, by returning from Mecca with Muslim teachers, lawyers, and builders. These traditions were recorded in the *Timbuktu Tarikhs,* which were chronicles of West African history, that were written in Arabic during the 1500s and 1600s.

Branched sword
The design of this sword, in terms of both its shape and the decorated blade, is typically Arabic. However, it was actually made in Chad in West Africa.

Dogon village
In the heart of modern Mali, the Dogon people live in houses poised on the steep cliffs of the Bandiagara Cliffs. Dogon history records their attempt to escape conquest by the empires of Ghana, Mali, and Songhay.

© DIAGRAM

Kanem Bornu

The Sultanate of Borno, the successor state to Kanem, once existed to the north and northeast of Lake Chad. Now part of present-day Chad, the sultanate was ruled by a dynasty which was founded 1,100 years ago, and lasted unbroken for 900 years. A representative of this dynasty lives on in the leader of the emirate of Borno – present-day Nigeria – and, to the present day, remains an important traditional leader there.

The region has been inhabited since around 1000 BCE; at first, by hunter-gathers who also fished and used tools made from bone and stone. Then, during the first millennium CE, the people were cattle herders (pastoralists) who lived a nomadic existence – they were not settled but moved from place to place in search of fresh pasture and water for their herds.

According to tradition a great Arab hero named Saif bin Dhu Yazan lived in the Yemen in the sixth century. He traveled to North Africa, and then south of the Sahara to Kanem, where he founded the Saifawa dynasty. The first definite evidence of the dynasty dates from the tenth century, when the people believed the king was divine. In the words of one Arab visitor: *"Their religion is the worship of their kings, for they believe that they bring life and death, sickness and health."*

By the end of the eleventh century, Kanem was an Islamic state but its kings were still considered divine. Its nomadic peoples had merged into a distinct group speaking one language, the Kanuri.

Kanem expanded greatly, but the state was plagued by internal disputes and battles with the Bulala, to the southeast. The Kanuri were finally driven out of Kanem by the Bulala, but they retreated to their southernmost province, Borno, to the west of Lake Chad.

Under Mai (King) Ali Gaji (died 1503), the Kanuri managed to reestablish their empire. Kanem was eventually taken, but the heart of the sultanate remained in Borno. The state was often simply called Borno (rather than Kanem Borno) during this second period. Under Mai Idris Alooma (1569–1603), Borno became the most powerful

Borno cavalryman (left)
Kanem Borno used cavalry to control trade routes. The horses were not native to the region, but had to be imported across the Sahara.

Foot soldier (right)
A Borno soldier from the 1800s still relied on his lance, or bow, in battle. Not all were equipped with firearms.

Royal procession (left)
A nineteenth-century engraving records the passage of the sultan of Borno through a regional capital.

Caged sultan
At public appearances in the 19th century the sultan gave an audience from a cagelike pavilion.

empire *in West Africa, and a center of Islamic learning and scholarship.*

The mais *lost their power after Fulani jihadists drove them from their capital in 1808. An Islamic scholar named El Kanemi helped the* mai *reclaim his throne in 1837, but became more powerful than the* mai, *using the title* shehu. *From 1846, after the last* mai *and his son were executed, the* shehu *ruled Kanem Borno.*

Borno survived colonialism, but only in Nigeria, where the emirate of Borno still exists.

Greatest extent (right)
The Kanuri-speaking inhabitants of Kanem conquered many non-Kanuri people, the sultanate reaching its greatest extent in 1230. Then, the northernmost lands crossed the Sahara, almost reaching the Mediterranean Sea.

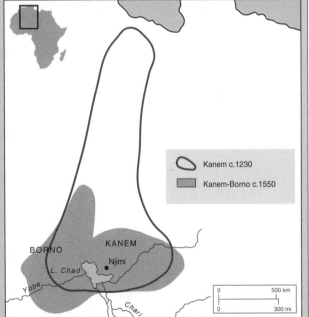

Kanem c.1230
Kanem-Borno c.1550

BORNO
KANEM
Njimi
L. Chad
Yobe
Chari

0 — 500 km
0 — 300 mi

© DIAGRAM

SONGHAY AND ITS NEIGHBORS

After the decline of Mali in the 1400s, states that had existed within its huge borders regained their independence. The most successful of these was Songhay. The Mossi, Hausa, and Tuareg people also founded long-lasting nations.

The kingdom of Songhay (or Songhai) was founded more than 1,250 years ago. It first emerged on the Niger River, in what is now the modern nation of Mali, around 750 CE. Its capital was most probably the important trading center of Gao, and profitable trade routes passed through its territory. Today, Songhay-speaking people still live in the region.

At various periods, Songhay was part of the ancient empires of Ghana in the 10th and 11th centuries, and Mali. The latter was overlord to Songhay for nearly 100 years, from around 1240 to 1337. During that time, to ensure their obedience to the conquerors, Songhay princes were often held hostage at the court of the current *mansa* (king) of Mali. There, it is reported in the 16th-and 17th-century *Timbuktu Tarikhs*, members of the Songhay royal family learned about kingship and empire building. At some time, two brothers of the Songhay royal family were employed (by force) at the *mansa*'s court as officers in the Mali army. They escaped from the court and returned home to Gao. The result was a revival of the Songhay monarchy. The kings of Songhay adopted a new title, *sunni* (or *sonni*), and took back control of their kingdom from Mali.

Sunni Ali

Songhay first rose to greatness during the 28-year reign of Sunni Ali, who reigned from 1464 to 1492 CE. He began by seizing Timbuktu from the desert-dwelling Tuareg people in 1469. The Tuareg had themselves wrested control of this vital trading depot from the Mali empire. Four years later, in 1473, he had captured Jenne, a busy trading city in the inland delta of the Niger River, and also once part of Mali. By the time of his death, Sunni Ali had made the Songhay empire the most powerful empire in West Africa. He is remembered as a great hero among the Songhay people of today.

Sankoré Mosque (left)
Under Askia Muhammad the princes of Songhay were educated in West Africa's first university which was located within the walls of the famed Sankoré Mosque in Timbuktu.

Early Songhay (below)
In the 1330s, Mali was the largest empire in West Africa, and Songhay was part of Mali. After 1337, however, Mali began to contract, and Songhay began to expand. By 1475, Songhay was bigger than Mali, which was becoming less politically important. Songhay reached its greatest extent in 1515.

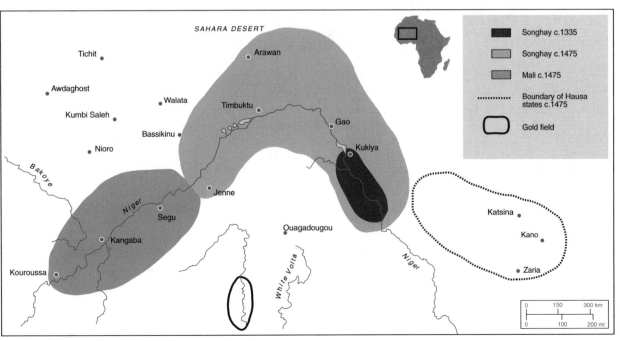

SAHARA DESERT

Tichit
Arawan
Awdaghost
Walata
Kumbi Saleh
Timbuktu
Gao
Bassikinu
Kukiya
Nioro
Jenne
Bakoye
Niger
Segu
Katsina
Kangaba
Ouagadougou
Kano
Kouroussa
White Volta
Niger
Zaria

Legend:
- Songhay c.1335
- Songhay c.1475
- Mali c.1475
- Boundary of Hausa states c.1475
- Gold field

0   150   300 km
0   100   200 mi

© DIAGRAM

Songhay – growth and decline of an empire

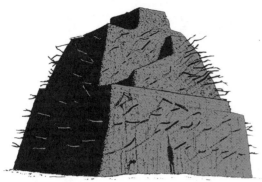

Tomb of Askia Muhammad
The tomb of Askia Muhammad still survives in Mali. It is a popular place for Islamic scholars to visit, and also for those interested in the history of the region. He was a devout Muslim, and Islamic learning and scholarship flourished under the Askia dynasty.

Songhay reached its greatest extent under Askia Muhammad (reigned 1493–1528), who built on the gains made by Sunni Ali's lifetime of military campaigns. Under Muhammad it reached an east–west extent that matched that of Mali at its peak, but Songhay extended much farther north, including the Tuareg's desert town of Aïr, as well as the salt deposits at Taghaza and Taoudenni, which were also situated in the desert to the north. Askia Muhammad was removed from the throne by his own sons in 1528.

Invaders

In 1591 the armies of the kingdom of Morocco swooped down from North Africa and conquered Songhay. The rulers of Songhay were left with a small kingdom around Dendi. The Moroccans tried unsuccessfully to control the large Songhay empire through a succession of puppet Songhay rulers whom they had installed at Timbuktu. However, these pashas were not successful rulers, and the last one died in 1621, reputedly by poisoning.

Tuareg warriors
Following the conquest of the Songhay Empire by the armies of the kingdom of Morocco, the Tuareg became more influential in the Niger region in West Africa.

48

Neighbors

While Songhay dominated the Niger Bend, the Mossi people to the south established seven states between the 1200s and the 1400s. The Mossi were not rich and made their living through the slave trade. With their cavalry, they went on regular raids against their neighbors to capture slaves. To the east of Songhay, Hausa states emerged. During the 1400s, the independent Sultanate of Aïr emerged from bands of Tuareg traders in the 1400s.

Economy

Songhay existed at the same time as ancient Ghana and, in a similar way, had from early days benefited greatly from the trans-Saharan trade. Ghana controlled the caravan routes leading to the north and west from the bend in Niger River, while Songhay controlled those leading to the north and east.

Songhay lost control of these trade routes to Mali, but later regained them after its decline.

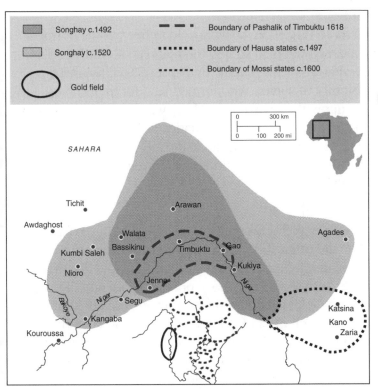

Legend:
- Songhay c.1492
- Songhay c.1520
- Gold field
- Boundary of Pashalik of Timbuktu 1618
- Boundary of Hausa states c.1497
- Boundary of Mossi states c.1600

SAHARA

0   300 km
0   100   200 mi

Tichit
Awdaghost
Walata
Bassikinu
Kumbi Saleh
Nioro
Arawan
Timbuktu
Gao
Kukiya
Agades
Jenne
Segu
Kangaba
Kouroussa
Katsina
Kano
Zaria
Niger
Bakoye

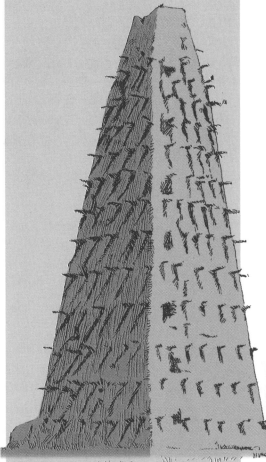

Minaret at Agadez, Niger
This tower, made from mud and wood, stands in Agadez, which was once the capital of the Tuareg Sultanate of Aïr. The sultanate was conquered by Songhay and then Kanem, but it survived to reach its greatest extent in the 1800s.

States
While Songhay dominated the Niger Bend, farther south the Mossi people created seven states between the 1200s and the 1400s. Legend says that the Mossi kingdoms were founded by a cavalry group that invaded from the south (what is now north Ghana).

© DIAGRAM

Askia Muhammad established an effective government in the Songhay Empire, dividing his realm into provinces ruled by governors. In the western, Mande-speaking, half of his empire, he ruled through armies of slaves who had been captured during wafare.

Songhay-speaking people were the most numerous people along the great bend of the Niger River. Even outside their state's changing borders, they were the largest ethnic group at some places, such as Jenne and Timbuktu. They were the boatbuilders, the fishermen, and the river traders of the region.

Ways of life

Some, like the Mossi to the south, were horse breeders. Green and fertile eastern Songhay was perfectly suited to horse breeding, unlike the dense forests to the south and the dry lands farther north. Mounted soldiers carrying lances, often highly-born nobles, were much feared members of the Songhay army. Some used the horses to make their raids for slaves more effective.

Slavery

In those times, slaves were sold to free people or trans-Saharan traders to supply the markets of North Africa, Arabia, and Europe. The emperor of Songhay kept colonies of slaves, who farmed land for themselves, and to supply the royal court. Many were born slaves because the children of slaves automatically became slaves; if a free woman married a slave, the king had the right to buy her children. Some children were even sold to buy horses for the cavalry.

Spread of Islam

Many people of Songhay adopted Islam, but even those who did often still practiced aspects of their original, African religions. Some historians think the divisions at court between those who supported Islam and those who did not helped weaken the empire, eventually allowing the easy conquest of Songhay by the Moroccan invaders. Sunni Ali was Muslim in name but is remembered as a champion of the non-Muslims within Songhay. He was hostile to the Muslim scholars and religious men of the

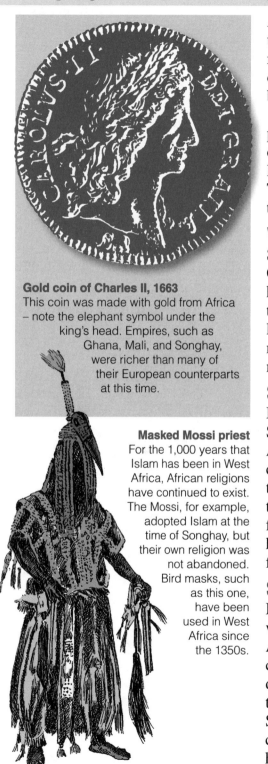

Gold coin of Charles II, 1663
This coin was made with gold from Africa – note the elephant symbol under the king's head. Empires, such as Ghana, Mali, and Songhay, were richer than many of their European counterparts at this time.

Masked Mossi priest
For the 1,000 years that Islam has been in West Africa, African religions have continued to exist. The Mossi, for example, adopted Islam at the time of Songhay, but their own religion was not abandoned. Bird masks, such as this one, have been used in West Africa since the 1350s.

major towns, such as Timbuktu, who were viewed as supporters of Mali. Under the Askias, however, Islam was promoted as a way of unifying the diverse peoples under Songhay's rule.

Religious life

Despite these conflicts, Islam flourished in the region during this era. Under the Askias, the mosques at Timbuktu and Jenne were again important centers of learning and worship. Scholars traveled to them from far away, and some families brought their children up to be men of learning and religion. In a section of a Timbuktu chronicle that relates the exile of religious men and scholars from the city by Sunni Ali, the chronicler also reveals how these families raised their children:

"On the day they left Timbuktu you could see grown men with beards anxious to mount a camel but trembling before it . . . for our . . . forefathers used to keep their children indoors until they grew up. Hence they had no understanding of practical matters, since they did not play in their youth."

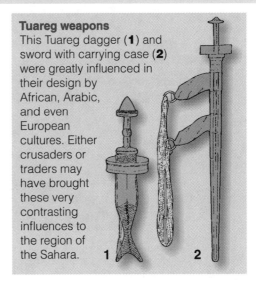

Tuareg weapons
This Tuareg dagger (**1**) and sword with carrying case (**2**) were greatly influenced in their design by African, Arabic, and even European cultures. Either crusaders or traders may have brought these very contrasting influences to the region of the Sahara. **1**   **2**

Timbuktu (below)
Timbuktu had long been a major town and Islamic center and it became even more so under the Askia dynasty. It was well placed for trade: European glass, North African pottery, and salt made its way across the desert to Timbuktu, then on the Niger River.

© DIAGRAM

The Seven True Towns

Kano walls (above)

This is a section of the adobe walls, as seen from the inside, that once surrounded the city of Kano. All the Hausa *Bakwai* were encircled by walls.

Hausa town (right)

Each of the Hausa states was based around a walled town called a *birane*. The towns were independent from each other, and each had its own ruling royal family. Inside the town lived traders and the weavers, dyers, and leather workers for which the Hausa were so well known.

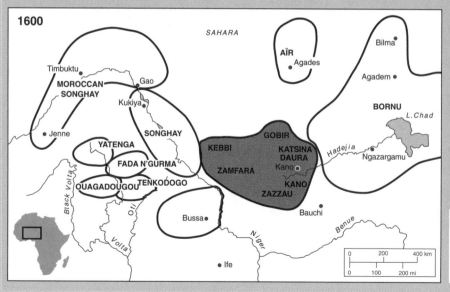

Hausa states and neighbors, c.1600 CE

At this time, Songhay had lost its northern provinces to the Moroccans, and its power had been shattered. However, Borno, which lay to the east of the Hausa, was still strong. The Hausa's contact with the gold-mining Akan people to the south was vital to the maintainance of both their wealth and trade.

According to tradition, the rulers of the Seven True Towns established by the Hausa in what is now northern Nigeria descend from a founding hero named Bayinjida, who became sarki *(king) of Daura after killing a monstrous snake and marrying the queen of Daura.*

The towns, or Hausa Bakwai, *which still exist today, are Biram, Daura, Gobir, Kano, Katsina, Rano, and Zaria (also called Zazzau or Zegzeg). Other powerful towns, such as Zamfara, Kebbi, Yauri, and Nupe also existed. Some of these towns, such as Kano, were home to men of learning who recorded the histories of these states in the form of chronicles. The Kano Chronicle, which survives today in a 19th-century Arabic manuscript, is one such history.*

By the start of the second millennium, several Hausa societies had been established in the region, and by 1350 states had emerged. They profited from the trans-Saharan trade routes that ran to the east of Songhay. Tuareg traders imported horses, weapons,

salt, copper, and pottery from North Africa. In return, the Hausa exported large quantities of cloth, leather, slaves, and ivory.

In the 1400s, Kano, Katsina, and Zaria embarked on periods of expansion. They imported large numbers of horses and huge amounts of weaponry from the Tuareg traders to the north. Zaria, then called Zazzau, was most powerful in the late 1500s under Queen Amina; even Kano and Katsina paid her tribute.

Though protected by their strong walls and cavalry, the Hausa were threatened by the powerful states of Kanem-Borno to the east and Songhay to the west. They spent much of the 1500s dominated by Songhay, then by Kanem. Later they were caught up in the Fulani jihads *that swept West Africa in the 18th century.*

The Hausa Bakwai, *and other Hausa towns, have survived to the present day, however, and the Hausa emirs are often significant figures in modern Nigerian politics.*

Qur'an

This miniature version of the Muslim holy book, dating from the late 17th or early 18th century, was made by Hausa people. The ruling classes among the Hausa were introduced to Islam by Dyula traders during the time of the Mali Empire, and the religion gradually became more widespread.

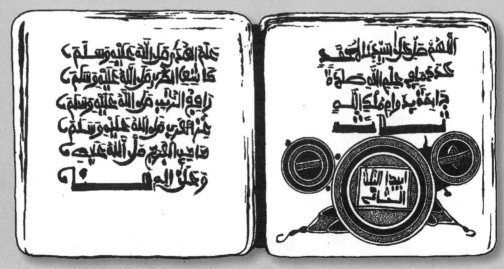

© DIAGRAM

KINGDOMS OF THE FORESTS

While the mighty empires of the savanna – Ghana, Mali, and Songhay – formed some of the most powerful West African states ever, the forested lands to the south, and along the coast, were definitely not backwaters. Long before the arrival of Europeans, states flourished in the forests and their fringes.

For many decades, historians thought that the forested regions of West Africa were quiet backwaters which were hardly affected by long-distance trade until the arrival of Europeans from the 1400s onward. The kingdoms of Benin, Ibadan, Dahomey, and Asante were well known to Europeans but, at the time, it was thought, erroneously, that they had emerged in response to the arrival of European traders on the coast.

A history of pre-European trade

Far from being cut-off from trading, there have in the past been vital regional networks and links to the trans-Saharan trade routes to the north via states, such as the Mossi kingdoms, and Songhay and Mali. Indeed, many of the goldfields so vital to the trade across the Sahara were located in the forests far south of the desert. Few, if any, states were founded simply in response to the arrival of trading Europeans, though trade along the coast did help many to flourish.

Maritime trade (below)
Long before the arrival of Europeans, West Africans traveled up and down the coast, and along inland waterways by means of canoe. This was the main mode of transportation in forested regions with rivers.

Forest workers (right)
This is a view of the rain forest of the Ivory Coast in the 19th century. Men work hard to cut down plants to make a path through the dense undergrowth.

Kingdoms of the forests – foundation and growth

Benin, Oyo, and Nupe, 1600

All three states had been in existence for at least 300 years by this time. Benin expanded greatly under the *oba* (king) Eware from the mid-1400s. Nupe dominated Oyo in the 1500s and fought with Benin, but Oyo broke away from Nupe's control in the 1600s. This century was one of expansion for Oyo, which grew southward to take advantage of trade with Europeans along the coast, and it also managed to dominate Nupe to the north.

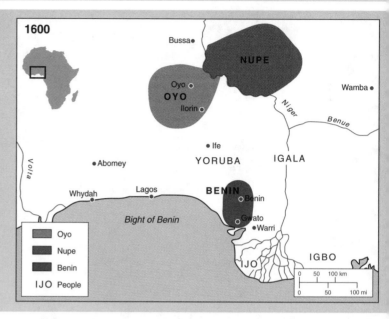

1600

Bussa•
NUPE
Oyo○
OYO
Ilorin○
Wamba•
Niger
Benue
•Ife
•Abomey
YORUBA
IGALA
Whydah•
Lagos•
BENIN
○Benin
Bight of Benin
○Gwato
•Warri
IJO
IGBO
0 50 100 km
0 50 100 mi
Oyo
Nupe
Benin
IJO People

Wheel-like Ife

This plan of the ancient city of Ife, now replaced by modern Ile-Ife (Nigeria), reveals the wheel-like structure which was common to Yoruba towns. The single lines represent earlier walls, and the double ones later walls.

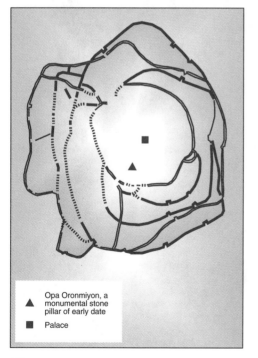

▲ Opa Oronmiyon, a monumental stone pillar of early date

■ Palace

It is difficult to know exactly when civilizations first emerged in the forested regions. There are few written records or ancient wooden structures, and artifacts have crumbled in the humid conditions. Igbo Ukwu is one of the earliest yet known.

Evidence of states has been provided by Europeans themselves. In 1507, for example, a Portuguese visitor to the (now Nigerian) Ijebu described it as "a very large city." Obviously, this and other places already had a history stretching back further than such initial sightings.

Ife

According to tradition, the first Yoruba kingdom to emerge was Ife. It was the capital of a kingdom by the 11th century, and the city itself was probably founded in the late first millennium. The Yoruba people still live in the region today, which is now in southwestern Nigeria.

The 14th century was a period of great prosperity for Ife, and many of the famous works of art associated with Ife date from this era. More than 20 heads are known from Ife, made of terracotta (pottery) and alloys of copper. Their style is incredibly realistic (termed naturalistic) and beautifully worked. The heads might be death masks of the *onis* (kings) of Ife; that is, realistic

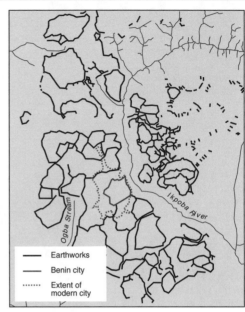

Yoruba states and Benin, 1730
By 1700, Oyo was the most powerful of the increasing number of Yoruba kingdoms, perhaps even the most powerful state in West Africa. It was often in conflict with the slave-raiding state of Dahomey, but conquered it in 1748.

Benin earthworks
The earthwork enclosures of ancient Benin spread far beyond the modern city walls.

representations of their heads to enable relatives to remember them after death.

Nupe

By the 1300s, Ife had been joined by the kingdom of Oyo, to the north of the forest's edge. North of the Niger River, the Nupe people founded their own kingdom sometime before 1500. The southward spread of both cavalry warfare and slave raids of the Hausa forced Nupe to reorganize into a centralized state. Nupe took slaves from the northern Igbo (of what is now southeastern Nigeria) and, by the 1500s, it was at war with Benin.

Oyo

Nupe was raiding the Yoruba towns and cities and, around 1535, it occupied Oyo. The *alafin* (king) and his court took refuge at Borgu, a neighboring kingdom. Eighty years later, with cavalry, they retook Oyo. In the 1600s and 1700s, Oyo became an empire.

Benin city walls
The city walls enclosed the *Oba*'s palace within successive rings. The complex wall system divides the land into the individual village sections that made up the city.

© DIAGRAM

The kingdom of Benin

To the southwest of Ife, the kingdom of Benin was founded sometime before 1300. The dynasties of Ife and Benin are remembered back to the 1200s, but both cities existed before then, perhaps as early as 900. Benin was not a Yoruba kingdom, though its famous bronzes might have been influenced by the Ife cultural tradition. Edo-speaking people, renamed Bini by an oba (king), were the subjects of Benin, though legend informs us that a Yoruba prince established the kingdom.

By the 15th century, Benin was surrounded by massive earthern walls and ditches, reaching up to 54 ft (17.5 m) tall and 7 miles (11.6 km) long. This indicates that Benin had a powerful central authority. Historians have estimated that it would have taken 5,000 men working 10 hours a day to complete the wall in one dry season, or 1,000 men over 5 dry seasons. Even more impressive are the earthworks,

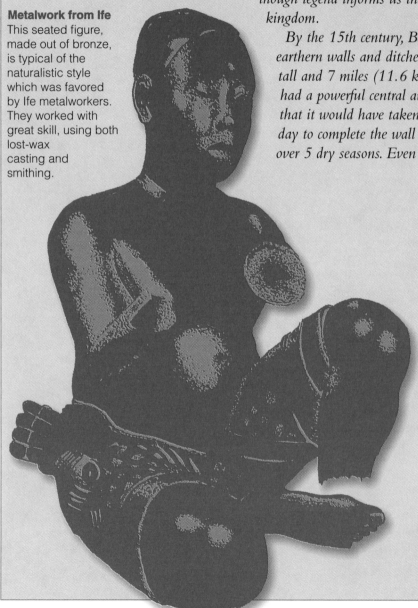
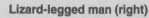

Metalwork from Ife
This seated figure, made out of bronze, is typical of the naturalistic style which was favored by Ife metalworkers. They worked with great skill, using both lost-wax casting and smithing.

Lizard-legged man (right)
Fish-or lizard-legged men holding their own legs have been a feature in Yoruba art since before the 1670s. This motif is most similar to ones used in ancient Rome (from 100 BCE to 300 CE), and in Europe from the 1100s, perhaps proving ancient links between these regions.

***Oni* of Ife (far right)**
This casting is of an *oni* (king) of Ife. The Yoruba kings were both political rulers and religious leaders, who conducted some important religious ceremonies themselves. This *oni* is wearing the clothing and carrying the regalia that was typical of the early rulers of Ife.

or iya, covering more than 1,000 square miles (2,600 sq km), which date from the 1200s to the 1800s. Consisting of earthern mounds enclosing patches of land, they might be evidence of smaller towns and villages that were swallowed up by Benin.

In the mid-15th century, Eware was the oba of Benin. He is remembered as the first of the great conquering obas, and Benin expanded under him. When the British conquered Benin in 1897, they ransacked the capital and looted many of the famous bronzes, which were, in fact, brass alloys of copper and zinc. Many were carried off to museums in Britain, or sold to finance wars.

Royal art of Benin
Much of Benin's art was concerned with royalty, especially the *oba* (king). The plaque (above left), made in the 1500s, shows the *oba* of Benin with his wife, and a tame leopard cub – a symbol of kingship. The ivory sistrum (above right) was a rattle-like musical instrument, containing bells on the inside, played at court. The spotted leopard (below), carved in ivory and covered in copper spots, is one of a pair used as water vessels. Water was poured from the mouth over the *oba's* hands in cleansing rituals.

Benin and the Yoruba kingdoms became wealthy through trading in ivory, palm oil, yams, kola nuts, peppers, and cloth with other African peoples. For Benin and Ife to produce their beautiful "bronzes," copper must have been imported from the north because there were no local supplies.

Trade with Europe

Benin sold pepper to the Portuguese sailors along the coast after the 1400s, asking for firearms in return which the Portuguese refused to supply. Slaves were rarely sold as their labor was needed in the kingdom, and trade with Europe languished for about 200 years.

Internal strife

Oyo took advantage of the slave trade with Europeans to expand southward toward the end of the 1700s, taking control of the trade routes that linked with the coast.

The Dahomey kingdom rose up, however, and challenged Oyo on its southern borders. Further wars occurred along the so-called slave coast in the 1700s. Oyo eventually conquered Dahomey in 1748, and gained control of the trade.

Glass–making

Ife specialized in the production of blue *segi* beads, which decorated the crowns of all the *alafins* (kings). Glass foundries produced hundreds of these beads a year.

Living off the forest

Most people made their living from the land. Sometimes they made a surplus to trade but, at other times, they only just managed to feed their families. The forest provided sustenance, including: wood for building and fuel, and with

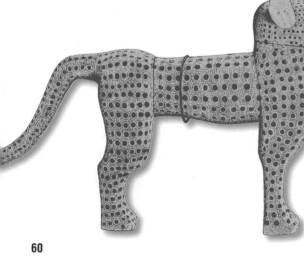

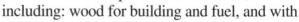

Bronze heads
The crowned head from Ife (left) was made between the 12th and early 16th centuries; the head (right) dates from 15th- or 16th-century Benin. Some heads, such as the example from Ife, were probably designed as portraits of deceased kings or chiefs. The hair and facial marks of the Benin head suggest that he was a foreigner; it might also have been the "trophy head" of a vanquished man.

which to make potash and charcoal (for metalworking); fish from its many rivers; beeswax and honey; sticky gum; rope made from vinelike lianas; and gold and iron ore. Crops, such as yams and oil palms, had also been farmed in the forest for thousands of years.

Forest land

When Europeans first visited the coast of West Africa in the 1400s, they described what they saw as impenetrable forest which cloaked whole coastal regions, especially near the equator. They thought people must live in clearings within untamed forest.

However, what they did not realize was that most of the forested land was either farmland, fallow land, or "wild" forest. The soil of the tropical forests was fertile if allowed to rest for long periods between farming. During these fallow periods, the forest would gradually reclaim the land.

Cattle were not important, since few could resist the cow-killing tsetse fly which thrived in the forests.

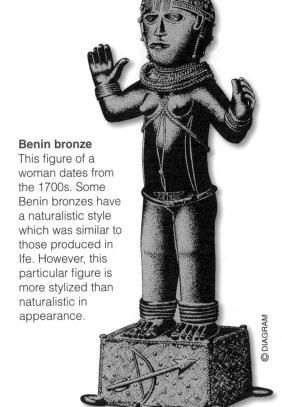

Benin bronze
This figure of a woman dates from the 1700s. Some Benin bronzes have a naturalistic style which was similar to those produced in Ife. However, this particular figure is more stylized than naturalistic in appearance.

©DIAGRAM

Kingdoms of the forests – society and politics

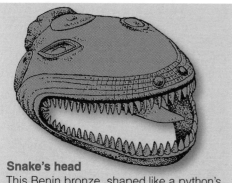

Snake's head
This Benin bronze, shaped like a python's head, dates from the 1700s.

The Yoruba people have long lived in dense, permanent settlements. While seemingly older cities have been unearthed to the north of the forests, such as Jenne-jeno, the Yoruba have been described as the most urban of all African peoples historically. Unusually for urban areas most of the people living in Yoruba towns and cities were farmers, although many were craftspeople or traders. Farmlands lay outside the city walls, and farmers lived within the wheel-shaped city, traveling on foot to tend their lands outside the city walls.

Political structures

The kings' powers were generally limited by town and palace officials in both Benin and the Yoruba kingdoms. In Oyo, the town chiefs commanded the capital's army and, at times, they were more powerful than the actual kings themselves. In fact, they made the kings into

Ibadan, c.1850
At this time, Ibadan was already a large city, and also the capital of the Yoruba Empire.

virtual puppets during the 1750s and 1760s. At times, the king could appoint an heir to his throne, but the custom was for the crown prince to commit suicide on the death of the king, and for a new king to be chosen by the palace officials and town chiefs.

The separate "villages" that made up Benin City each had their own chief, and the *ogiso* was the most important of these. The *ogiso* and his *uzama* – the village chiefs – limited the power of the *oba* (king). If an *oba* was seen to be particularly incompetent, he might even be ritually killed by the officials. In one near-disastrous civil war in Benin at the end of the 17th century, the *oba* emerged with his authority intact by playing the palace chiefs off against the *uzama*.

Headless societies

Not every society in the region was based around centralized political structures like these. The Igbo, in particular, have long been known for their democratically organized "headless societies" in which anyone had access to power, and people advanced through merit and achievement. The Igbo lands lay to the southeast of the Niger–Benue junction, and they were densely settled in self-governing villages, or federations of villages, by the time of Oyo and Benin.

Ivory tusk
Carved elephant tusks, such as the one ilustrated (right), were often inserted into bronze heads representing *obas* (kings) of Benin, and became part of the royal shrine. The heads, with their elaborately-carved tusks, acted as memorials to past *obas*.

At the court of the king
King Atiba receives the Anglican missionaries, Townsend and Mann, at Oyo in 1853.

Benin, c.1600s
The first European visitors to Benin described it as a 'great city,' similar in size and buildings to those in Portugal.

© DIAGRAM

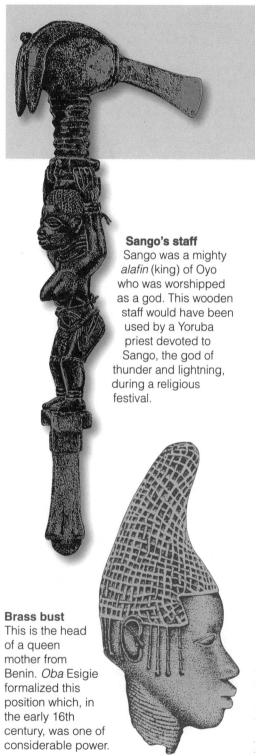

Ivory amulet
Elaborately carved with great skill, this bracelet, or cuff, was made for the royal court of Benin. It is one of a pair, and is 5.5 inches (14 cm) high. The court maintained specialist craftworkers to produce artifacts that formed the king's regalia, and made up the royal shrine, where prayers and gifts were offered to ancestors.

Sango's staff
Sango was a mighty *alafin* (king) of Oyo who was worshipped as a god. This wooden staff would have been used by a Yoruba priest devoted to Sango, the god of thunder and lightning, during a religious festival.

Brass bust
This is the head of a queen mother from Benin. *Oba* Esigie formalized this position which, in the early 16th century, was one of considerable power.

Islamic belief never really took hold in the forests of West Africa. Despite the natural resources of the forests, life could be hard there. Insect-borne diseases, such as malaria, sleeping sickness, and river blindness, were common, because the insects bred in the many rivers.

African beliefs

People approached their own gods to help when someone was ill, and in dealing with troubles, but they also remembered them when things were fine. Although every language group had its own unique religion, they shared some features. Most religions involved showing great respect to the spirits of dead ancestors, who could aid or hinder their living relatives. While they did not have the absolute power of divine beings, the kings of Benin and the Yoruba were seen as important points of contact with the spiritual world.

Yoruban gods

The Yoruba developed a range of gods, with each one tending to a different sphere of worldly life. They named the city Ife after Ifa, the god of divination, who persuaded the heavenly prince Oduduwa to climb down to Earth at the site of the city, so they regard Ife as the birthplace of humankind. Oranmiyan, a grandson or son of Oduduwa, is said to have founded Benin and then Oyo. Other legends say that, with death approaching, Oduduwa divided his kingdom between his sons. Sango, the god of thunder, was originally a legendary king of Oyo who was said to be able to control the thunder and lightning. Yoruba myth says that he became too proud of his powers, however, and as he was demonstrating his abilities, he destroyed his palace, wives, and children by mistake. The king committed suicide in shame. Worship of Sango became the state religion in Oyo.

Human sacrifice

Evidence of human sacrifice dates from the 1200s in Benin. The *oba* himself would conduct the most important religious ceremonies, at which sometimes one or more people might be sacrificed so that they could carry a message to the gods. When a king was buried, or even ritually murdered, his servants might be buried with him.

Roles of men and women

Men were the heads of households, and custom allowed them to marry as many wives as they could support. Women were responsible for feeding and taking care of their children, and shared the task of feeding their husbands with their co-wives. Women grew their own food to do this, and often traded surplus produce or goods. Drier forests experienced a long dry season, when little rain would fall. Then, it was the onerous task of women and children to walk several miles a day to bring water home for cooking, washing, and drinking.

Royal women were important; kings often lived secluded lives, rarely leaving the palace, where they lived with hundreds of royal wives and the queen mother, who was responsible for training the heir to the throne.

A rare appearance in public
The *oba* (king) of Benin City rarely appeared in public, and then only if shrouded in an elaborate costume that included a beaded coral crown. In Nigeria today, the *oba* is still an important figure on the current political scene.

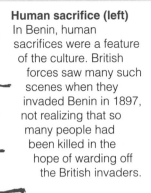

Human sacrifice (left)
In Benin, human sacrifices were a feature of the culture. British forces saw many such scenes when they invaded Benin in 1897, not realizing that so many people had been killed in the hope of warding off the British invaders.

Oranmiyan's staff (right)
This huge, carved, granite stone stands today in Ife. Prince Oranmiyan, a legendary figure in Yoruban history, is said to have used it to drive Ife's enemies away.

© DIAGRAM

ERA OF FIREARMS AND THE SLAVE TRADE

European involvement: 1400–1650

1400s CE	Wolof dominate what is now central Senegal
1470	Portuguese mariners reach the uninhabited islands of São Tomé and Príncipe. Kingdoms of Akan-speaking people exist along Gold Coast
1471	Portuguese mariners reach coast of modern Ghana
1482	Portuguese establish first fort at El Mina
1485	The first European settlers arrive on São Tomé and Príncipe, triggering a demand for enslaved Africans to work on sugar plantations
1492	Columbus reaches America
by 1500	Dyula people's Kong kingdom exists. Fon people's kingdom of Allada (Arda) in existence. Fulani settled in Futa Toro (northern Senegal), and Futa Djallon (Guinea)
1517	Spain approves import of slaves to the Caribbean
1550s	At least 24,000 ounces (680 kg) of gold are being traded with Portuguese each year
1576	Africans destroy Portuguese fort at what is now Accra
1600s	Many European nations engage in the Atlantic slave trade.
c.1610	Abomey is settled.
c.1620	Dako founds dynasty at Abomey (Dahomey)
1620s	Dutch West India Company is founded to profit from slave trade
c.1640	Wegbaja rules over Dahomey
1650s	Segu and Kaarta founded

The years from 1500 to 1800 are sometimes known as the era of firearms and the slave trade. Europeans first arrived on the coast of West Africa in the late 1400s, bringing firearms with them, and many states in West Africa profited from the resulting gold and slave trades.

The impact of Europe

When the first European sailors arrived on the coast of West Africa in the 1400s, there was no sudden change in the region. In fact, for the West Africans, the arrival was hardly of interest. States and kingdoms looked to the north, focusing on the lucrative trade routes that had crossed the Sahara for many hundreds of years. Over the course of several centuries, however, the impact Europeans had on the region was huge.

In response to increasing demands for slaves and gold along the coast, West African states shifted their attention south. At times, wars became more common as empires struggled to control the lucrative trade routes and depots, or raided for slaves. Slavery was not new to the region, but it intensified greatly in response to European and, later, American demands.

Most kingdoms were established long before the Europeans had arrived, but many flourished with the new trade opportunities, while others suffered greatly at the hands of slave raiders and slave traders. Before the 1500s, the most powerful West African kingdoms

Benin bronze, c.1600 (right)
The Portuguese were responsible for introducing firearms to the coastal states of West Africa.

were located farther inland, either in the forests or the savanna, and not immediately along the coast. Partly in response to increased trade, kingdoms near the coast, such as Dahomey and the Asante Kingdom, grew more powerful at times than those located inland.

First arrivals

In the 1400s, European nations, following the example of Portugal, were looking for ways to trade directly with the people who supplied them with imports; in the case of West Africa this was, at first, primarily gold. This would also mean that the Europeans would not have to pay the Arabs who normally served as middlemen in this trade. Also, as the Europeans saw it, there was much honor associated with being a great sea-faring nation, and riches could be made by extending the boundaries of trade.

The Portuguese colonized the islands of São Tomé and Príncipe off the west coast of Africa in the 1480s. They planned to grow sugar in large plantations, but also wanted cheap labor to make their crops more profitable. In return, the African traders received cheap iron, cloth, coral, copper, brass, and, perhaps most importantly, firearms. These weapons allowed more effective slave raids to be carried out.

By the end of the 1600s, England, France, Denmark, the Netherlands, Portugal, Spain, and Sweden were engaged in the Atlantic slave trade.

European involvement: 1651–1850	
1660s	Denkyira is the major Akan state
1670s	Denkyira and Akwamu are major Akan powers. Fulani launch *jihads* to establish states
c.1680–1717	Osei Tutu is king of the Asante Empire
1680–1730	Oyo and Dahomey frequently at war, with Oyo dominant
c.1685–1708	Akaba is king of Dahomey Empire
1698–1701	Asante destroy Denkyira in fight for freedom
1700s	Opposition to slavery and the slave trade develops
c.1708–1740	Agaja's reign over Dahomey
1726	Fulani people establish Muslim state of Futa Djallon
by 1727	Dahomey conquers Allada and Whydah
1730	Akwamu breaks up
1748	Oyo conquers Dahomey
1750	Opuku Ware, king of the Asante Empire, dies
1750s	Slave trade at its height
1754	Kaarta is founded
1764–1777	Osei Kwadwo is king of the Asante Empire
1791	Nupe breaks away from Oyo
1792	Freetown established for freed slaves (Sierre Leone)
1824	Asante defeat British
1806–1807	Asante conquer Fante people of coastal lands
1807	Britain abolishes slave trade
1808	US abolishes slave trade
1818	Dahomey breaks free from crumbling Oyo Empire
1850s	Al Hajj Umar launches *jihads* on Bambara kingdoms of Kaarta and Segu, thus founding Tukulor Empire

El Mina (the mine)
The first Portuguese fort on the West African coast, this was established in 1482.

© DIAGRAM

Akan states

Yam festival, Kumasi, 1817
The *asantehene* (king) and his court, shaded by
umbrellas, parade at the annual Yam Festival.

In the forests along what came to be known as
the Gold Coast (now the coast of Ghana and
neighboring nations), Akan-speaking people
had established small kingdoms by the 1470s.
This region earned its name as a result of the
lucrative gold trade based around the goldfields
that lay within 80 to 150 miles (130 to 240 km)
from the coast. The Akan people had migrated
into the region from the northern fringes of the
forest zone.

The struggle for control

From the 1660s, various Akan states struggled
for control of this region. Based around cities,
such as Denkyira, Kumasi, Accra, and
Akwamu, each was ruled by its own king.

Two kingdoms, Denkyira and Akwamu,
came to dominate the region. Threatened by
these major powers, the northern Akan
speakers, the Asante (or Ashanti), formed a
union based around Kumasi. All the kings
agreed to accept the king of Kumasi in the
role of overlord (*asantehene*) in order to

protect their interests. In the 1680s, under the
first *asantehene* Osei Tutu (reigned
c.1670–1717), the emerging Asante empire
gained control of the lands between them and
the coast. The kings of conquered Akan states
had to show loyalty to, and acknowledge the
supreme authority of, the golden stool – a
symbol of Kumasi overlordship that,
according to legend, "came from the sky."
Between 1698 and 1701 the Asante fought
Denkyira for independence, supported by
Akwamu. Denkyira fell apart. Akwamu then
broke up after an attack in 1730, leaving the
Asante empire as the major power in the
region. They conquered the Mossi Dagomba
kingdom to the north and, in 1765, they made
the first attempt to conquer the coastal lands
of the Fante Akan people. The Fante were
finally conquered by 1807, and Asante
controlled all the lands to the coast.
The Asante remained powerful until defeated
by the British at the turn of the century.

Necklace (right)
This intricately-worked gold necklace was made at the height of the Asante empire in the 1700s.

Golden casket (below)
The figures on the lid of this brass casket are of the *asantehene* (king) and his courtiers. It would have been used as a store for gold dust.

Gold weights (left)
The Asante made small brass weights to measure the gold dust and nuggets that were so vital to their kingdom's wealth.

© DIAGRAM

Fon states

The Fon people live mainly in the southern half of what is now the modern state of Benin, which has no relationship to the historic kingdom of Benin. Then known as the Aja, by 1500 they had established the kingdom of Allada (otherwise known as Arda).

An offshoot of the Allada royal family settled land to the north around Abomey (Dahomey) in about 1610. The emerging state's first kings, Dako, Wegbaja, Akaba, and then Agaja established a highly centralized and military state that controlled most of the land behind the coastal states by the start of the next century. The years between 1680 and 1730 were ones of almost constant war between the Aja states and between Oyo and Dahomey, resulting in the supply of many captives to the slave trade at the rate of about 18,000 to 20,000 every year. At that time Agaja (reigned c. 1708–1740) was the Dahomey king; he is remembered as a great statesmen and conqueror. The Dahomeans finally conquered Allada and the kingdom of Whydah (Ouidah) by 1727. For much of that century, Dahomey was still forced to

A Dahomean king
Agaja reigned from c.1708–1740. He established a regular, trained army, employed spies to infiltrate enemy forces, and was also responsible for creating the famous corps of women warriors, better known as Amazons.

War dance
Asante warriors prepare for battle in a ritual dance.

pay tribute to Oyo, however, but managed to remain largely in control of its own affairs. Once Dahomey controlled the coastal regions, only the officials of the king were allowed to take part in the slave trade. The number of slaves sold fell dramatically, to a level high enough to maintain the supply of firearms and court luxuries. Ports other than Whydah, such as Porto Novo, became new centers of the trade, although Dahomean ports were far from dead. Dahomey broke free from the then crumbling Oyo in 1818 for good.

Dahomey's army

Armies in West Africa were often temporary creations brought together for a specific war or campaign. Dahomey was one of the few African states to have a permanent army. By the mid-1800s, it numbered more than 12,000 well-trained and well-equipped soldiers. Of these, several thousand were women – the famed Amazons of Dahomey.

A display of wealth

For major festivals, a huge tent was erected in the courtyard of the the king of Dahomey's palace. It was fixed to the ground by large iron nails, since wood would rot over a period of time. The king was seated inside the tent so that he could watch the parades of women carrying provisions, and the ranks of soldiers passing by during this celebration of his wealth.

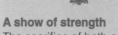

A show of strength

The sacrifice of both animals and humans, at the behest of the king, was a feature of life in Dahomey c.1850.

Western Atlantic states

Western states, 1700

Kong was founded by the Dyula trading people sometime after 1500 CE. Bobo-Dioulasso was another Dyula kingdom in control of important trade routes between the gold fields and the savanna. Kaarta and Segu were powerful Bambara states.

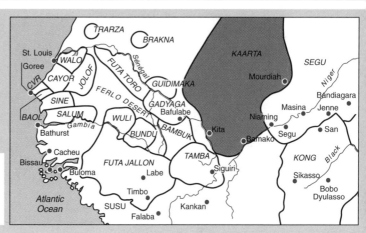

BUNDU	Empire, kingdom, or state
SUSU	People
——	Boundary of state
	Bambara states

| 0 | 150 | 300 km |
| 0 | 100 | 200 mi |

Wolof trader, c.1800

Along the Western Atlantic coast of Africa a new class of traders emerged, who would use their wealth to give them power and social standing.

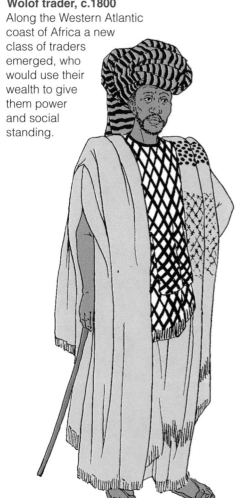

Away from the southern coastal regions, in the tropical grasslands to the north, the kingdom established by Wolof traders in the 1200s dominated what is now Senegal in the 1400s. It was ruled by an elected leader called the *burba*. As trade with Europeans on the coast became more important, its power disintegrated.

In the savanna to the east, Bambara people established two states after the break up of Songhay: Segu and Kaarta. According to tradition, the brothers Barama and Nia Ngolo founded the kingdoms around 1650. Kaarta probably has a more recent origin dating from the mid-1700s. Both states were powerful in the region. In the early 1800s, Segu lost Jenne and Timbuktu to Seku Ahmadu from Macina, and then Al Hajj Umar, the founder of the Tukulor empire, conquered Segu.

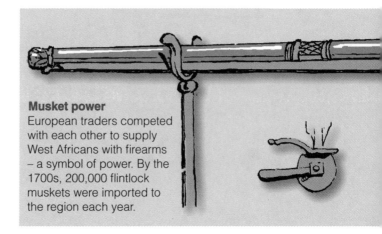

Musket power

European traders competed with each other to supply West Africans with firearms – a symbol of power. By the 1700s, 200,000 flintlock muskets were imported to the region each year.

Economy

When the Portuguese arrived on the coast of West Africa, they sought to control the gold trade, and wanted to prevent the Africans from trading with any passing ship. So, they made deals with leaders that allowed them to establish forts on their land in return for traded goods. The Africans viewed this as a rental arrangement, or as the payment of tribute, but the Portuguese saw their forts as overseas possessions of the crown. Gold was collected and stored at these forts, where Portuguese officials and soldiers lived. The main role of the forts was not to extend control over the Africans, but to prevent other European nations trading there. This pattern of fortified settlements was typical of European nations who sought to maintain a presence on the coast of West Africa.

In an attempt to make converts, the Portuguese refused to sell guns to non-Christians, but the British, Danes, and Dutch obliged. The Benin kingdom refused to accept the Portuguese terms, although they had plenty of slaves to sell. In the 1500s, restrictions on the sale of slaves to the Portuguese were put in place, and virtually none were sold to them for 200 years. However, Benin still sold slaves to other African nations.

Ivory art (right)
African artisans created items, such as this carved ivory salt cellar from Benin, for royal courts in Europe.

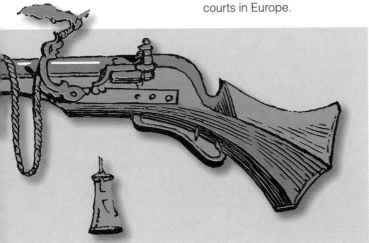

© DIAGRAM

The slave trade

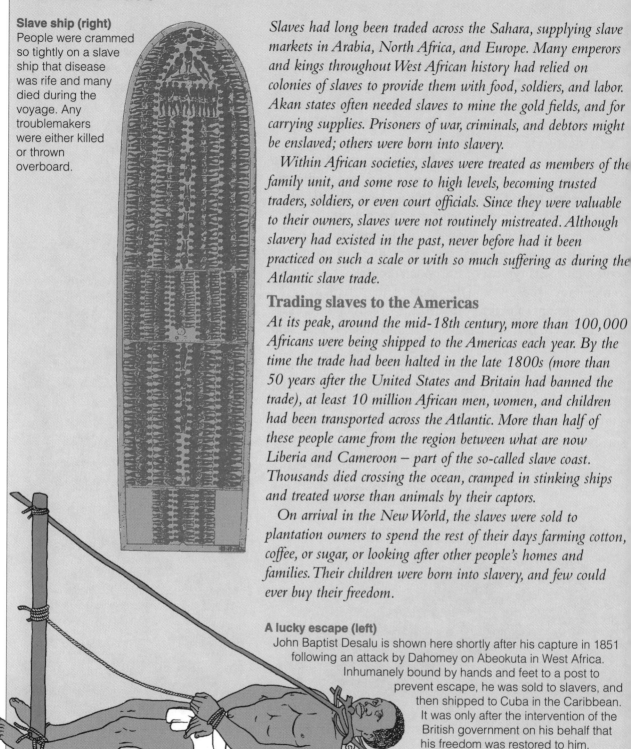

Slave ship (right)
People were crammed so tightly on a slave ship that disease was rife and many died during the voyage. Any troublemakers were either killed or thrown overboard.

Slaves had long been traded across the Sahara, supplying slave markets in Arabia, North Africa, and Europe. Many emperors and kings throughout West African history had relied on colonies of slaves to provide them with food, soldiers, and labor. Akan states often needed slaves to mine the gold fields, and for carrying supplies. Prisoners of war, criminals, and debtors might be enslaved; others were born into slavery.

Within African societies, slaves were treated as members of the family unit, and some rose to high levels, becoming trusted traders, soldiers, or even court officials. Since they were valuable to their owners, slaves were not routinely mistreated. Although slavery had existed in the past, never before had it been practiced on such a scale or with so much suffering as during the Atlantic slave trade.

Trading slaves to the Americas

At its peak, around the mid-18th century, more than 100,000 Africans were being shipped to the Americas each year. By the time the trade had been halted in the late 1800s (more than 50 years after the United States and Britain had banned the trade), at least 10 million African men, women, and children had been transported across the Atlantic. More than half of these people came from the region between what are now Liberia and Cameroon — part of the so-called slave coast. Thousands died crossing the ocean, cramped in stinking ships and treated worse than animals by their captors.

On arrival in the New World, the slaves were sold to plantation owners to spend the rest of their days farming cotton, coffee, or sugar, or looking after other people's homes and families. Their children were born into slavery, and few could ever buy their freedom.

A lucky escape (left)
John Baptist Desalu is shown here shortly after his capture in 1851 following an attack by Dahomey on Abeokuta in West Africa. Inhumanely bound by hands and feet to a post to prevent escape, he was sold to slavers, and then shipped to Cuba in the Caribbean. It was only after the intervention of the British government on his behalf that his freedom was restored to him.

Long-term economic effects

The effects this trade had on West Africa have been long lasting and severe. The region lost millions of its most productive inhabitants — the healthiest young men and women were most in demand by the slavers. Wars were provoked to allow the capture of more slaves, and political stability was lost.

The overall shift in West Africa from an economic focus in the north on a long-established, stable, and profitable trans-Saharan trade, to a lucrative but unstable market in the south, had major implications for the region's long-term economy. This shift in focus was only strengthened during the following colonial era, when West Africa became even more reliant on world markets via its coastal ports. By then, the markets were even more unstable but no longer so lucrative, for West Africans anyway. Before this era, West Africa had been no more or less developed than other parts of the world. Several West African empires, at their peaks, could lay claim to being the largest in the world. After this era, however, Africa had fallen behind the world in measurable terms, such as per capita income, political stability, and health provision.

Dogon slave
This bronze figure, which was probably made by the Dogon people of modern Mali, depicts a man with his hands and ankles in chains. Those defeated in battle were often bound in this way, and then displayed in the village of the victorious army.

Ship's deck (left)
These men are being "loaded" on to a slave ship for a journey to the Americas that could take between three and six weeks.

Political structure and society

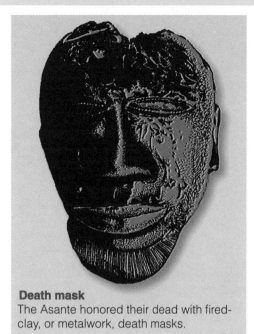

Death mask
The Asante honored their dead with fired-clay, or metalwork, death masks.

The Denkyira Empire had no administrative structure beyond the required payment of tribute by conquered kings. When too much tribute was demanded, the Asante kings rebelled, and founded the Asante Empire.

The Akwamu people, in contrast, sent members of the royal family to govern conquered lands. This was to ensure that the states were loyal to the center. However, the Akwamu princes often married into the local royal family, and made their state a power base from which to challenge the center. The governor of Accra, the uncle of the Akwamu king, made such a challenge in 1730, thus destroying the empire.

When he was king, Osei Kwadwo (reigned 1764–1777) introduced professional administrators to the Asante Empire. These police officers, soldiers, officials, and businessmen were unconnected with the traditional power structures, and only hired for their loyalty to the king. By creating a new power structure in this way, Osei Kwadwo allowed himself and his successors the real chance of increasing their control of an empire that began as a royal confederation.

Fon political structures

Allada was ruled by a king whose power depended on the support of the rulers of the smaller kingdoms that made up the state. Dahomey, however, was controlled directly by one powerful king, who ruled with the help of several ministers and officials. The two most important were the *tononu* and the *kangbodé*. The *tononu* was the most important man in the kingdom after the king. He was head of the palace, the king's mouthpiece, and the only person the king would speak directly to. The *kangbodé* controlled matters outside the palace.

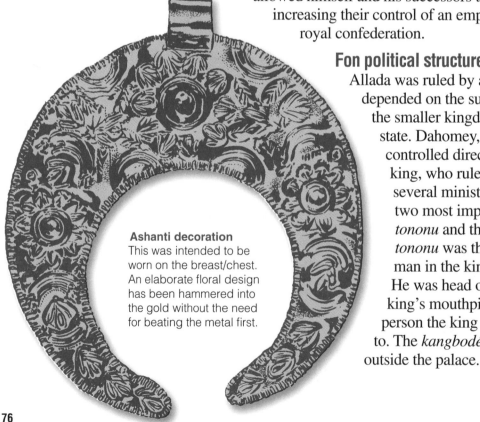

Ashanti decoration
This was intended to be worn on the breast/chest. An elaborate floral design has been hammered into the gold without the need for beating the metal first.

Men and women

Men were the rulers of most African kingdoms, but women still had access to a certain amount of power. Each of the king's officials was matched by a female counterpart. The tasks of the women were to monitor the men and their expenses, making sure that the officials remembered all their duties and performed them satisfactorily. Even the king had his match in the queen mother.

Royal wives

In Whydah, royal wives, of which there were hundreds for any one king, carried out punishments from time to time. They might be sent to destroy the house of a criminal or disloyal servant, or even to kill him or her. No one dared intervene. Sometimes the wives were sent to settle "little wars" between villages.

Most Fon kings had many wives; some reports say several thousand. A proportion of these were not true wives since their role was to look after the women who bore the king's children. All the royal wives lived with the king in the palace, which no ordinary man was allowed to enter. When the current king died, battles over succession would often break out – it was rarely a simple matter of the king's eldest son inheriting the throne. The successor needed to have some supporters among the wives, who often took sides in these disputes.

An official called the *kpakpa* recruited wives for the palace. Families were considered honored to be able to offer a daughter to the palace. Other reports tell how troublesome and badly-behaved women were given to the king. For many women, becoming a royal wife was preferable to simply being the wife of a commoner, which involved few privileges and much toil.

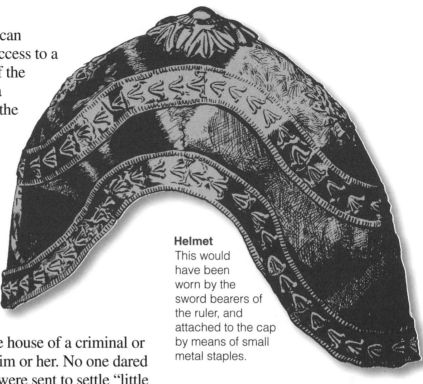

Helmet
This would have been worn by the sword bearers of the ruler, and attached to the cap by means of small metal staples.

Royal pipe
Intended for display only, these gold objects were carried by the king's servants on public occasions.

© DIAGRAM

77

The Amazons of Dahomey

Elephant hunters (below)
Amazons were skillful hunters. They fixed antelope horns to their heads for disguise, encircled their prey, and then moved in, hopefully, for the kill.

From all around the world, legends tell of women warriors as feared, as strong, and as brave as people thought only men could be. Ancient Greek myths tell of a race of female warriors called Amazons. Few of these legends are based on fact, apart, that is, from the famed Amazons of Dahomey.

Origins
In the 1600s, King Wegbaja formed a band of female elephant hunters. They supplied the court with ivory and meat. Historians of Dahomey say that the oldest Amazon fighting unit, the gbeto, had its origins in such hunters. In the 1700s, armed women were guarding the king and his palace. No men other than the king and a couple of high-ranking ministers were allowed in the palace, so the women were crucial to his safety. In 1729, when Agaja was king, women soldiers fought in an attack on newly conquered Whydah. This is the first time that these soldiers are known for sure to have appeared in battle. Agaja formed Amazon units, each with their own colors, and chose officers to whom he gave symbols of rank.

Many women from wealthy families were in the Amazon troops, alongside slaves who owed their privileged position to the king. A few were actually born as Amazons. All were very loyal, and honored to serve the king.

Training
Each Amazon was given a young girl to serve her; in return, the Amazon taught her charge how to fight and become a soldier. The children would accompany the soldiers into battle, carrying their weapons for them. These young girls grew up to become Amazons, eventually replacing their

Spoils of war (right)
This musketeer carries a severed male head and a flintlock musket. A club and dagger are tucked into her belt. On the skullcap is an image of a crocodile, the symbol of her troop or perhaps valor in battle. Her blue and white striped clothes were common battle dress in the Amazon army.

Officers, c.1850
These two Amazons are wearing silver horns on their heads, and bells around their necks, revealing that they are officers in the army.

...mistresses in the field. Amazon weapons included bow and arrow, musket, and huge razor-like blades. All were used with fearsome effectiveness in battle. As part of their training, Amazons performed mock battles, at which they would scale thorny fences taller than themselves, while ignoring the pain.

Palace life

Amazons were not part-time soldiers. From an early age they were trained in fighting and how to use weapons, to show courage in the face of danger, and, above all, to protect the king. Yet, they still had to work to pay their way. They lived in dormitory-like barracks inside the palace that the women made themselves. The king contributed to the cost of their food and clothes, but the amount depended on his wealth at the time, and it was rarely enough to meet all their needs. Instead, the women farmed, made goods within the palace, and traded provisions to acquire the things they needed. Higher-ranking Amazons had women slaves to help them with tasks.

Although Amazons counted among royal wives, few became royal partners. In principle, the women were not allowed to marry or have lovers. If they did, they might be sold into slavery or executed. Some were allowed to retire and start families as a reward for courage in battle, or were given in marriage to men who had served the king well.

© DIAGRAM

Fulani *jihads*

The Fulani people of West Africa are descended from Africans who originated from both north and south of the Sahara. Today, they live mainly in the areas of central Mali, northern Nigeria, southern Niger, southwestern Chad, Senegal, southern Mauritania, Gambia, and also Guinea.

In the past, they were a nomadic people, who traveled great distances in the dry grasslands and semideserts of the Sahel in search of water and pasture for their herds of cattle. They played a major part in the history of West Africa, actively spreading Islam throughout the region and resisting French and British colonial rule for a number of decades.

From the 700s, Fulanis migrated into the above regions. They came from Morocco, but their origins beyond there are not known. Most settled around Futa Toro in northern Senegal; while others moved farther east and south, to Futa Djallon and northern Nigeria. By the 1400s they were very well established, living in scattered communities.

Senegalese soldiers (above)
These African soldiers in the French colonial army fought against the armies of Al Hajj Umar.

Cavalry (left)
Fulani cavalry of the 18th and 19th centuries refused to use guns, claiming they were fit only for slaves.

Jihad

The Fulani carried on a series of jihads *(Islamic holy wars), which started in the 1670s. Most* jihads *were organized in an attempt to overthrow non-Fulani rulers who were taxing everyone excessively and pressurizing them to pay rents, and to provide services to the rulers. At first, most Fulani were not Muslim, but a class of educated Fulani scholars lived in the towns; these were often the leaders of* jihads, *and the founders of Muslim states.*

One of the most powerful of these states was that founded by the Muslim scholar Usman dan Fodio (1754–1817). He lived in the Hausa state of Gobir, where he amassed a following who helped him carve out the Sokoto Caliphate, or Fulani Empire, which was actually a joint Fulani-Hausa state. Sokoto was conquered by the British in 1903.

To the west of Sokoto, Al Hajj Umar (1797–1864), a Fulani Muslim scholar, established the Tukulor empire in the mid-1850s, which was based at Futa Djallon. Umar had spent 12 years at Sokoto, and had already made the obligatory pilgrimage (hajj) *to Mecca.*

Umar's successor, Seku Ahmadu, spent much of his reign resisting the French, but he was eventually defeated by the end of 1894.

Fulani states and *jihads*
Sokoto reached its greatest extent in 1830. To the west of Sokoto, Macina was established as an independent *jihad* state by 1827. By 1860, within 10 years of its foundation, Al Hajj Umar's armies had conquered an empire – the Tukulor empire – to the west of Macina. Though vast, the empire was not stable and included many non-Muslims who resented Tukulor rule. Together, the Sokoto and Tukulor empires ensured that Islam became the major religion in the northern part of West Africa at that time. the maps (below) show the extent of the Fulani states at the following times: (**1**) 1800; (**2**) 1860; and (**3**) 1885.

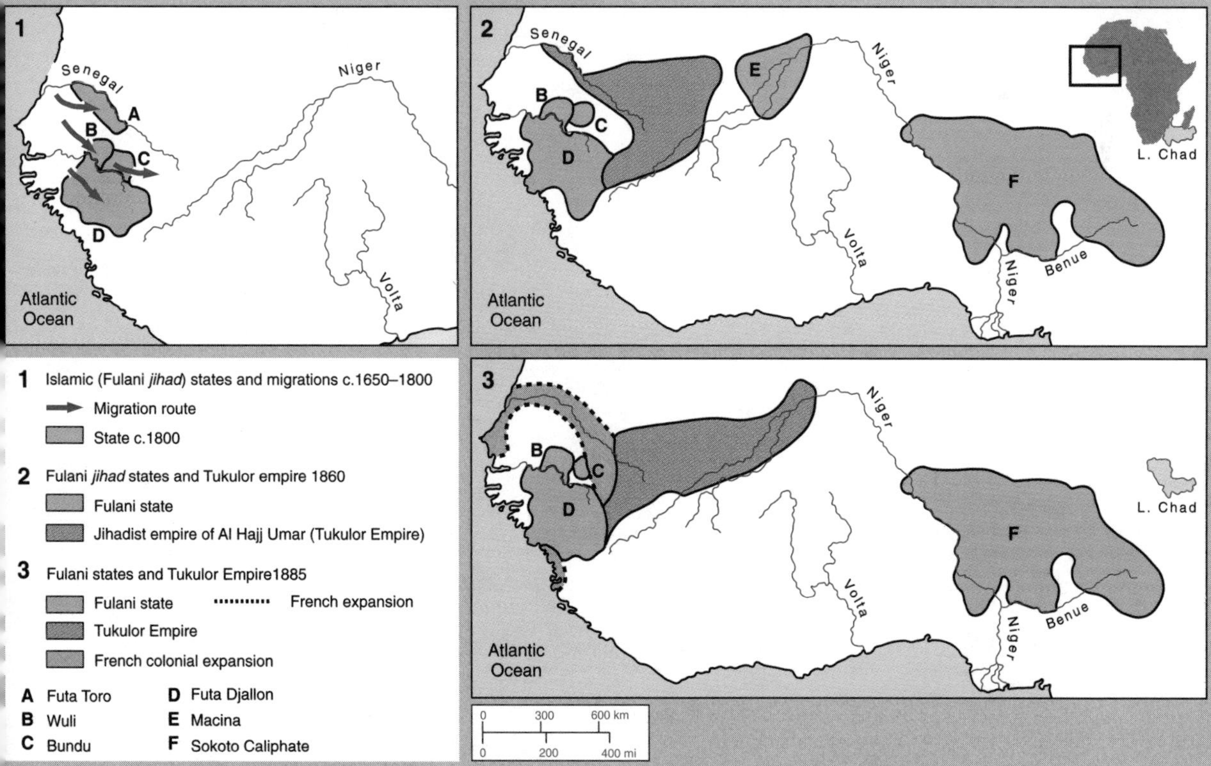
1
Senegal
Niger
A
B
C
D
Volta
Atlantic Ocean
2
Senegal
Niger
B
C
D
E
F
L. Chad
Volta
Niger
Benue
Atlantic Ocean
3
Niger
B
C
D
F
L. Chad
Volta
Niger
Benue
Atlantic Ocean
1 Islamic (Fulani *jihad*) states and migrations c.1650–1800
Migration route
State c.1800
2 Fulani *jihad* states and Tukulor empire 1860
Fulani state
Jihadist empire of Al Hajj Umar (Tukulor Empire)
3 Fulani states and Tukulor Empire1885
Fulani state
French expansion
Tukulor Empire
French colonial expansion
A Futa Toro
B Wuli
C Bundu
D Futa Djallon
E Macina
F Sokoto Caliphate
0 300 600 km
0 200 400 mi

FROM "SCRAMBLE" TO COLONIAL ERA

Colonial involvement: 1792–1861

1792	Settlement of freed slaves established at Freetown, Sierra Leone, by Britain
1795	Scottish explorer Mungo Park arrives in West Africa
1800s	Christian missionaries from Europe begin to establish themselves in coastal lands
1807	Britain abolishes slave trade. Sierra Leone becomes a British colony
1808	US abolishes slave trade
1818	France abolishes slave trade
1824	Asante defeat British
1826	Asante resist British in Second Anglo-Asante War; coastal Fante fall to British and become Gold Coast colony
1843	The French reoccupy their fort at Whydah (Dahomey)
1847	Republic of Liberia declared for freed slaves from US
1850s	Trade in palm oil more important than slave trade
1851	Britain destroys Lagos
1861	Lagos made a British colony

A Scotsman in Africa
Mungo Park (1771–1806) was born in Scotland but died in West Africa. He made two expeditions to Africa to search for the source of the Niger River and thus open up the region to more direct trade with the European colonial powers. In this illustration he is shown in the middle of a group of African women, all of whom are intrigued by his European clothes.

Historians often talk of the "scramble" for Africa, a period toward the end of the 19th century when European states were rushing to take control of nations throughout Africa. Typically, the starting date for this period is given as the Berlin Conference of 1884–1885.

At that conference, European nations set down rules concerning the colonization of Africa. They agreed to inform each other of any territory that they wanted to claim, and then make the claim good by occupation, thus establishing a colony. The Niger River (and the Congo in Central Africa) were to remain open to all. Within 30 years of the conference, the process of carving Africa up into chunks of European territory had been completed.

The first colonies

In reality, the desire to acquire territory in Africa started before the late 1800s. France and Britain had both

stablished colonies before that date. By 1833 Britain had mall colonies in Gambia and Sierra Leone (Freetown); nd France had four small colonies in Senegal. The scramble" was not triggered by one event, but rather by nany different processes that combined to change the uture of Africa forever during the 1800s.

he causes of colonization

he most important reasons for colonization were ramatic changes in trading patterns, the abolition of lavery, and the economic effects of the Industrial evolution. Gradually European nations preferred to ade in goods other than people, to control the markets, nd the suppliers themselves. The fundamental motive vas simple: the colonizers thought they could make noney from their colonies.

Colonial involvement: 1863–1918	
1863–	Asante defeated in Third and
1874	Fourth Anglo-Asante Wars
1865	Slavery abolished in US
1860s	Slave trade comes to an end
1874–	World depression forces fall
1896	in prices of African goods
1884–	Berlin Conference held to
1885	establish rules of colonization
1893	Tukolor defeated by French
1895	France forms French West Africa colony
1896	Asante made a British colony
1897	Ibadan and Benin (southern Nigeria) conquered by British
1901	French end Mossi resistance
1902	Asante joined to Gold Coast
1903	British conquer Sokoto. French conquer Mauritania
1906	Sultanate of Wadai (eastern Chad) is conquered, bringing all of West Africa except Liberia under colonial rule
1914–	During World War I West
1918	Africans fight on both sides. France and Britain defeat Germany in Togoland

Two European explorers
René Caillié (far left) made an exploratory journey to West Africa which lasted from 1827–1828, while Heinrich Barth (left) later explored the region during the period 1850–1856.

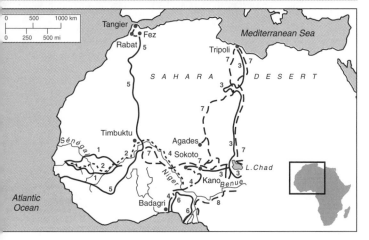

Exploring Africa

This map shows the locations of the major explorations of Africa during the period 1795–1856. British, French, and German explorers were as follows:

1 Mungo Park, 1795–1797
2 Mungo Park, 1805–1806
3 Hugh Clapperton, Dixon Denham, and Walter Oudney, 1822–1825
4 Hugh Clapperton and Richard Lander, 1825–1827
5 René Caillié, 1827–1828
6 Richard and John Lander, 1830
7 Heinrich Barth, 1850–1856
8 William Baikie, 1854

©DIAGRAM

Ending the slave trade – political factors

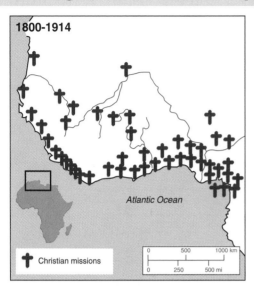

Christianity in West Africa, 1800–1900
Missionary activity was most successful in areas of West Africa that had suffered greatly from the slave trade. For example, local communities that had been torn apart by the loss of some of their members.

Antislavery patrol, 1851
The British, once the most involved in the slave trade among non-African nations, were perhaps the best-equipped to end it. In this illustration, an antislavery patrol destroys Lagos (modern Nigeria) on the grounds that it was a base for the slave trade. A decade later the British colonized Lagos.

During the 1700s, while the slave trade was at its awful height, people increasingly turned against the buying and selling of human beings. A revolution in France, and a civil war in Britain, had been fought for the rights of the common people, and also to end the absolute power of the monarchies.

A few churches and individuals had always been against the slave trade and slavery itself; others became convinced by the increasing numbers of antislavery campaigners. Among these campaigners were several educated ex-slaves, such as American-born Frederick Douglass and African-born Olaudah Equiano, both of whom proved eloquent and effective.

Religious leaders, ordinary people, politicians, and others campaigned for the end of the slave trade. They were often mocked, but had their first victory in Denmark, when slavery was outlawed in 1792. Other nations soon followed: France in 1794 (and then again in 1818), Britain in 1807, the United States in 1808, Sweden in 1813, and the Netherlands in 1814.

Political factors

Abolishing slavery and the slave trade was not enough, however, to bring them to an end. Slavery had long been practiced in Africa, as it had been elsewhere in the world. Land has never been in short supply in West Africa, but access to the labor of people has proved more difficult to

btain. Empire-building African kings often controlled arge territories, but their greater concern was to gain ontrol of large numbers of people. Without people to arm, rear animals, trade, and fight in their armies, nations ould not be powerful. To African kingdoms, the slave rade was in some ways a by-product of this need to naximize a kingdom's population. It explains why imply abolishing slavery and the slave trade did not ring the practices to an end in the region.

Europeans were unaware of the forces at work in African politics, though, and in the 1800s many argued hat ending the slave trade would bring an end to slavery n the region. When that did not happen, however, it was sed as yet another excuse to justify European conquest nd colonial rule of the region.

As long as there was a market in the Americas for laves, people would be sold and shipped across the Atlantic Ocean. Although numbers fell, the slave trade ontinued for decades after many nations had abolished it.

Slavers ran the risk of losing their expeditions to British avy patrols, however, and businesses were forced to look or other types of trade to remain profitable. Trade in alm oil was fostered and, in such places as southern Nigeria, it became more important than slave trading. Vhen the United States abolished slavery in 1865, the nd of the slave trade was near.

German missionary
Christian missionaries followed in the wake of European explorers. The information they supplied on the region to traders and politicians was vital to the process of opening up the region to trade and, eventually, colonization.

Bathurst, The Gambia
Sierra Leone was established as a refuge for freed slaves in the late 1700s. It then became the headquarters of British missionary activity in West Africa in the 1800s. Many freed slaves were settled at Freetown, and at other settlements nearby, such as Bathurst (now known as Banjul).

© DIAGRAM

Ending the slave trade – economic factors

The dancing fiddler
Billy Waters was a well-known busker outside a London theatre in the 1800s. Billy, and others like him, helped focus people's attention on the plight of former slaves.

Economic forces also helped to ensure the end of the slave trade. The Industrial Revolution began in England in the late 1700s but soon spread to other parts of the world. It was triggered by a series of inventions, resulting in powered machines (with steam engines, at first) that could be used to mass produce cloth, transport goods in bulk, and generally revolutionize industry.

Industrial growth
Britain developed large-scale manufacturing industries. For the first time, fabrics, goods, and even furniture could be made in large amounts. This growth in production led to a search for new markets into which to sell the goods, and sources of cheap raw materials from which to make them. Some people argued that industrial growth would stop if markets and supplies did not expand to cope. The traders of Europe, who already had extensive contacts with West Africa, knew where to look for them.

At first, the British government encouraged trade through independent businessmen but was not greatly interested in taking control of the markets and suppliers. The French government took a more active role sooner, launching campaigns to secure trade routes along the Sénégal River, for example.

Refuges for freed slaves
As the abolition of slavery movement gained momentum, many people were increasingly concerned about what would happen to freed slaves.

New communities were established on the West African coast as refuges for freed slaves: Freetown, Sierra Leone, by a British humanitarian group in the late 1700s; and Liberia (with its capital at Monrovia) in 1847 by the American Colonization Society, a white humanitarian group.

Freetown was settled by slaves freed by British antislavery patrols, as well as by ex-slaves from Britain and Jamaica. It was made a colony in 1807. Monrovia (right) was settled by ex-slaves from the US, some of whom had won their freedom fighting against the British in the American War of Independence.

Industrial decline

At the end of the 1800s, there was a depression in world trade. The price of palm oil, a major West African commodity, fell from around $250 per barrel, to less than $125. At those rates, there was very little profit for the Europeans. So, they looked for ways to cut out the African traders, and to gain direct access to producing areas inland from the coast.

Some argued that if Europeans controlled the production, supply, and trade of the goods, they could ensure profits. To achieve this goal, they needed to take political control.

Competition

There were other reasons for the ending of the slave trade that had very little to do with Africa itself. There was much rivalry in Europe in the 1800s, especially between Britain and France. These disputes spilled over into Africa. Neither France nor Britain would be outdone by the other, and every nation wanted to stop other European nations trading in the regions in which they had most influence. That could only be done if they controlled the traders, trade routes, and suppliers.

Sir George Goldie (above)
As head of the United Africa Company (UAC), he controlled the buying and selling prices of palm oil in the lower Niger region in the late 1800s.

Meeting with the king, 1819 (below)
Joseph Dupuis, British Consul to the Asante king, visited Kumasi to try and resolve a dispute between the king and the British Company of Merchants. The company was taken over by the British government a few years later with the dispute unresolved.

Resistance to colonialism

Samori Touré
Samori Touré, who was of Malinke origin, became a powerful symbol of resistance to colonial rule in the Niger region of West Africa in the 1890s. His empire was defeated by the French in 1898.

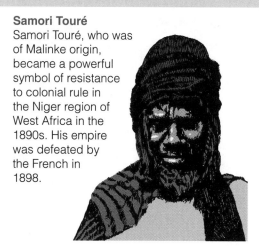

The European colonial powers made a major push for territory in Africa, but they were met with resistance every step of the way. This was particularly true of the Asante and Dahomey empires and among the decentralized Igbo people. In one case, 250 Asante fought off more than 4,000 British troops.

Some smaller states, and Ibo villagers, adopted guerrilla tactics, hiding out in the bush or forest, and attacking swiftly before troops had a chance to prepare. Their knowledge of the land gave them the advantage. The lack of one central leader did not prevent the Ibo being among the most difficult people to conquer.

Eventually superior European resources, such as weaponry (including newly-invented machine guns), supplies, and strength of numbers, brought them success.

Conflict with the French

The French concentrated on occupying large expanses of land inland from coastal regions. They hoped this would enable them to trade with, and tax, large numbers of people, not realizing that population levels were low in the dry savanna and semideserts.

In the 1890s, the French defeated the Tukulor empire, inspiring the British to defeat the Sokoto Caliphate to prevent further French expansion inland. By 1906 the whole region was under colonial rule apart from Liberia.

Conflict with the British

The British concentrated most of their efforts on the Gold Coast region, where trade was vital to many overseas British businesses. Several wars were fought with the powerful Asante (or Ashanti) empire, who controlled the Fante states along the coast. The Asante beat the British in the first battle, but were eventually defeated in 1874. They continued to rebel for several years afterward.

The Yoruba (southern Nigeria) were conquered by 1897, and Benin was sacked in the same year – the palace was burned down and thousands of works of art were taken by the British. Much of Nigeria was conquered by the Royal Niger Company.

Trophies of war
Crown Prince Bahadou, who became King Glele, is shown here with his father, King Gezo; together they reigned over Dahomey for 71 years. The king's drum is decorated with the heads of men killed by his troops in war. With their well-trained, fierce, and loyal army, the Dahomeans put up great resistance to the French. However, Dahomey was finally conquered in 1892.

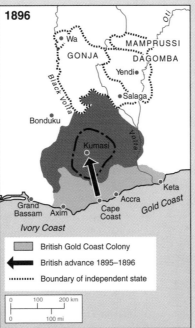

1831

Wa
MAMPRUSSI
GONJA
Yendi
DAGOMBA
Salaga
Black Volta
Volta
Oti
Bonduku
Kumasi
FANTE STATES
Accra
Lomé
Keta
Grand Bassam
Axim
Cape Coast
Gold Coast
Ivory Coast

- – – Boundary of Asante heartland
- ▉ Asante Empire
- ••••• Boundary of Fante states
- ▉ Area controlled by British 1831–1874
- GONJA State conquered by Asante

1896

Wa
MAMPRUSSI
GONJA
DAGOMBA
Yendi
Salaga
Black Volta
Volta
Oti
Bonduku
Kumasi
Keta
Accra
Gold Coast
Grand Bassam
Axim
Cape Coast
Ivory Coast

- ▉ British Gold Coast Colony
- ← British advance 1895–1896
- •••••••• Boundary of independent state

0   100   200 km
0   100 mi

Anglo-Asante Wars

There were four wars between the Asante and the British. In the first (1824), the British were defeated. After the second (1826), the coastal Fante states fell to the British, and became the Gold Coast colony. In the third (1863) and fourth (1874) wars, the Asante were defeated, and became part of the same colony in 1896. Rebellions continued until at least 1901. The map (far left) shows the the region in 1831, and the map (left) the situation in 1896.

Asante Expedition, 1873–1874

British troops were transported to the Gold Coast in West Africa from a convoy of ships. Teams of people were on hand to pull the rowing boats on to the shore, and to ensure minimal loss of life during the landing exercise.

A casualty of war

The death of Sir Charles McCarthy in the First Anglo-Asante War in 1824 was avenged by Colonel Sutherland. However, the British still lost this war, and had to wait until 1826 to restore their pride in the Second Anglo–Asante War.

© DIAGRAM

Society and politics

The two most important colonial powers in West Africa were Britain and France.

Contrasting colonial systems

The British colonies were ruled by governors who reported to the colonial minister in the British government. French governors reported to a governor-general based in Dakar (Senegal), who reported to the French government.

Networks of district officers were set up to implement policy at a local level. They ruled through African chiefs. These chiefs supported colonial rule, either because they had been given their rank by foreigners, or because they did not want to lose their power.

At this level, the French and British adopted different strategies. The French policy was one of direct rule – they selected chiefs to rule on their behalf, regardless of whether they had any claim to power. British officers, however, adopted a policy of indirect rule. They did not replace local political systems but used them to fulfil the aims of the colonial government – that is, as long as the political system did not act against them. The Asante, for example, were ruled directly for a while after they resisted British rule.

Sir Frederick, later Lord Lugard
While Governor for Northern Nigeria, he developed a theory of indirect rule. In 1912 he was given the task of amalgamating Northern and Southern Nigeria.

From Dakar to St Louis
The first French railroad to link the coastal areas with the River Niger was built in the 1880s. Both France and Britain built railroads in their colonies to transport goods to the coast with greater efficiency. Long-standing links with northern Africa, and internal trade networks, were ignored or neglected.

Legislative councils

The governors of British colonies were aided by legislative councils. These examined and approved laws, budgets, and policies, and included a few chosen representatives of local opinion, traders, and professionals. Such institutions had been set up in the 1800s, when these representatives were just as likely to be black as white.

In the 1900s, however, Africans were replaced by Europeans. People campaigned for elected African officials on these councils but with little success until the end of the colonial era.

African elites

Many educated Africans worked in the civil service, but only in the lower ranks. Their superiors were always Europeans, and Africans in the same positions as Europeans were paid less than their colleagues. Increasingly, as service in the civil service abroad emerged as a recognized career, these African officials were replaced with European civil servants.

Educated Africans, angry with their unfair treatment, were at the forefront of nationalist movements which were founded to campaign for the granting of self-rule.

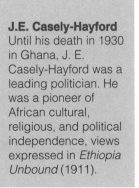

J.E. Casely-Hayford
Until his death in 1930 in Ghana, J. E. Casely-Hayford was a leading politician. He was a pioneer of African cultural, religious, and political independence, views expressed in *Ethiopia Unbound* (1911).

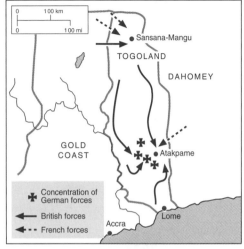

Concentration of German forces

British forces

French forces

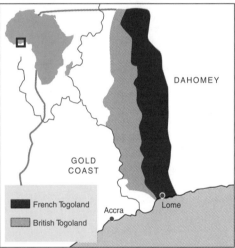

French Togoland

British Togoland

Dividing the spoils
During World War I, British and French troops occupied German Togoland and, in 1922, the League of Nations mandated the British to administer the western third of the territory, and France to govern the eastern two thirds. The map (top) shows the allied invasions (1914–1916), and the map (bottom) the mandated territories (1919–1922).

© DIAGRAM

91

The economy, culture and religion

Forced labor
This carved section of a wooden panel originates from a palace door of the Ogogo of Ikere Ekiti in Yorubaland, Nigeria. It shows Captain Ambrose, who was the first British District Commissioner, being carried in a hammock by two Africans in 1898.

Palm oil awaiting shipment
This illustration shows barrels of palm oil being loaded onto a ship in Nigeria, 1922. Palm oil replaced slaves as the main trading commodity of West Africa with Europe in the mid-1800s. Its price, however, went up and down to a great extent with market forces.

During the colonial era, West African economies were focused on cash crops. Cocoa, cotton, coffee, bananas, timber, rubber, palm oil, and groundnuts were the main crops. In some regions controlled by the French, farmers were forced to grow cash crops. The whole region became dependent on global markets, which has had serious consequences on the economies of these nations since they became independent.

Mining
European-owned mines made great profits from gold and tin in the Gold Coast (now Ghana) and Nigeria, and diamonds in Sierra Leone. Africans did not share in these profits and could only work down the mines.

Taxes
The most unpopular of colonial policies was taxation, such as the British-imposed hut tax (or poll tax). This was a *per capita* tax that could only be paid in cash. In French West Africa, even children were taxed. Taxes forced people to look for ways in which to raise money rather than concentrate on feeding their family. They were also used to force people to grow the cash crops Europeans required, and to work in the mines and other white-owned industries. Many people rose up against these taxes, but revolts were brutally put down by troops. Thousands of men migrated to the mines of the Gold Coast in an effort to earn money for taxes.

"Assimilation"

The French professed an aim to make all the people of their colonies French citizens, with the same rights and duties as those living back in France – this process was termed "assimilation."

However, by 1937, of the 15 million West Africans under French rule, only around 80,500 were citizens. The French authorities did not extend the right of equal status beyond a few thousand in their oldest colonies in Senegal. The majority of the people were not citizens but subjects. They had no effective political rights, and no right to appeal against official decisions.

Religion

Settlers from Monrovia and Freetown, who were known as Creoles, spread Christianity by visiting areas beyond Liberia and Senegal. While many adopted Christianity, it was often practiced alongside African religions.

Africans made use of the schools that missionaries established, and in some places an educated, Christian elite emerged. But, these people were shunned by colonial officials, and found it hard to find work suitable for their skills and education.

Senegalese woman
This late 19th-century lady is of mixed African and French parentage. French colonial policies encouraged people to adopt all things French, a process known at the time as assimilation.

Two distinguished West Africans
The first West African bishop, Samuel Ajayi Crowther (right) lived 1809–1891. He was a scholar and pioneer of the Yoruba language and history studies.

J. Africanus B. Horton (left) was a Creole surgeon and scholar from Sierra Leone. He qualified as a doctor and served as an officer in the British Army, later publishing books on a variety of medical and political subjects.

© DIAGRAM

The Women's War, 1929

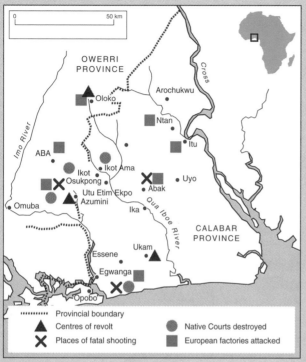

OWERRI PROVINCE

Oloko

Arochukwu

Cross

Ntan

Itu

Imo River

ABA

Ikot Ama

Ikot Osukpong

Uyo

Abak

Utu Etim Ekpo Azumini

Omuba

Ika

Qua Iboe River

CALABAR PROVINCE

Essene

Ukam

Egwanga

Opobo

········· Provincial boundary
▲ Centres of revolt
✕ Places of fatal shooting
● Native Courts destroyed
■ European factories attacked

War zone
This map shows the areas, primarily in the Calabar and Owerri provinces, in which the conflict occurred during the war in 1929.

Massacre at Egwanga Beach
On December 16, 1929, Calabar Province was declared a prohibited area. On that day, and without warning, British soldiers fired on unarmed women at Egwanga Beach, Opobo. Reports vary, but it is claimed that up to 500 women died that day.

In 1929, in what is now southeastern Nigeria, African women launched a revolution against British rule. It began with thousands of women demonstrating against rumored plans to tax them. They marched on towns and besieged government property, chanting war songs. Then, unarmed, they destroyed British-owned factories and the hated native courts which administered British rule through warrant chiefs. The protests swept across the entire Owerri and Calabar provinces, spread by networks of women's groups. The most severe disturbances were at Opobo, and more women lost their lives here than anywhere else.

Causes of the revolution
The Women's War was largely a result of colonial policies. The British generally practiced indirect rule. In regions that had no obvious single leader, however, they tried different tactics. The main inhabitants of the region caught up in the war were Igbo, but Ibibio women also rose up in Ukam and Essene areas to the southwest. The Igbo and Ibibio did not live in centralized societies. They had long lived in democratic, village-based communities led, when decisions were needed, by councils of elders. Among the Igbo, these elders were selected by the community from people considered to be successful and of good character. Women had several voices on

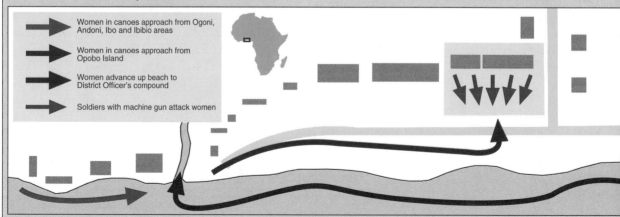

Women in canoes approach from Ogoni, Andoni, Ibo and Ibibio areas

Women in canoes approach from Opobo Island

Women advance up beach to District Officer's compound

Soldiers with machine gun attack women

the village council. They were selected by other women to protect their economic and political rights.

The British, however, thought that Igbo women had the same rights as their European counterparts, assuming their husbands would speak on their behalf. Warrant chiefs – always men who supported the colonial power – were chosen by the British from those they thought powerful enough to rule. The chiefs had no historical claim to power and went against long-standing systems of local government. The women were affected since their voices were not heard by the new rulers.

The economic lives of women were also affected. Women, not men, provided most of the food and clothes for their children through farming and trading. Despite organized protests, women lost control of local markets to traders of cheap European goods. The British controlled and monopolized trade. All these reasons increased, or created, financial dependence on men.

Riot or war?

These events have been referred to as the "Aba Women's Riot." However, the battles did not start, or peak, at Aba. Igbo women, however, called the events Ogu Umunwayi, and Ibibio women Ekong Iban, both meaning "Women's War."

The Women's War was a nationalist struggle on behalf of all their people, not just themselves. Direct taxation affected everyone, but it was women who had been denied all access to power structures – a situation to which they were far from accustomed. Colonial rule also forced women into a less equal position with men. They lost much of the power and economic independence they once enjoyed.

As a result of the war, British officials realized that the Igbo could not be governed by false chiefs, and they set up various levels of councils to replace the system of warrant chiefs and native courts.

Pottery altarpiece
Igbo men controlled the growing of yams, which played an important role in Igbo cultural and economic life. Yams were given as ritual and ceremonial payments. They also became important cash crops during the colonial era, giving men access to sources of cash otherwise denied to women.

NOTICE.

THOSE WHO SAY THAT WOMEN ARE TO BE TAXED ARE TELLING LIES.   WOMEN **ARE NOT** TO BE TAXED.

18/12/20.

K. V. Hauitsch,
Divisional Officer,
Ikot Ekpene.

NTÖT.

MBON EBOHO ETE KE EBO EBAN ENÖ OKPOHO A-TAX ESUKHÖ NSU. OWO IBOHO IBAN EKPE OKPOHO A-TAX.

18/12/20.

K. V. Hanitsch,
Divisional Officer,
Ikot Ekpene.

A colonial order
This poster attempted to dispel the rumors that women were to be taxed. The British taxed each adult man but, when rumors circulated that women were also to be taxed, open revolt broke out in the region.

© DIAGRAM

95

WEST AFRICA TODAY

Ahmadou Ahidjo
He led Cameroon to independence in 1960, and became its first president. Ahidjo succeeded in uniting the English- and French-speaking parts of the country before he went into exile in France in 1982.

Freedom
Cape Verde gained independence from Portugal in 1975, an occasion marked by the issue of this commemorative stamp.

Between 1957 and 1975 West Africa achieved independence from colonial rule. Since then many countries have experienced political instability. Ethnic and religious differences led to conflict, made worse by economic and environmental problems. Military coups and dictatorial one-party governments have also been features of the region.

One country that has suffered particularly badly from ethnic conflict has been Nigeria. It is a petroleum-rich country but conflict has kept the country poor. Sierra Leone and Liberia, too, have known civil wars, which have shattered their economies. By contrast, Cameroon and Senegal have enjoyed far greater political and economic stability. Ivory Coast was one of Africa's most successful countries until civil war broke out in 2002.

Cameroon

In 1960 Cameroon became independent from France. Southern Cameroons, formerly a British colony, joined Cameroon, which then became the Federal Republic of Cameroon. From 1966 the Cameroon National Union (CNU) became the only political party. In 1972 the country was renamed the United Republic of Cameroon, and a centralized government was set up. In 1982 it was renamed Republic of Cameroon.

Since 1977 Cameroon has exported oil, despite disputes with Nigeria, and has been relatively stable, using oil revenues to develop its economy. In 1982 Paul Biya became president. In 1997 he was reelected for seven years, appointing Peter Musonge as prime minister.

Cape Verde

Cape Verde gained independence from Portugal in 1975. The first president was Aristide Pereira of the African Party for the Independence of Guinea and Cape Verde (PAICG). Plans were made to merge with Guinea-Bissau, but a military coup in Guinea-Bissau in 1980 ended hopes of federation. Pereira's renamed African Party for the Independence of Cape Verde (PAICV) remained Cape Verde's only political party until 1990 when a multiparty democracy was introduced.

In 1991 the Movement for Democracy (MPD) defeated the PAICV, with Dr António Mascarenhas Monteiro becoming president. During the 1990s the government attempted to modernize the country with help from the International Monetary Fund. In 2001 the PAICV was reelected to power.

Chad

Chad became independent in 1960 and, since then, it has experienced military coups and almost continuous civil war. War first broke out in 1962 between a northern Muslim group – the National Liberation Front (FROLINAT) – backed by Libya from 1971, and the government, backed by France. Fighting continued but mainly between rival northern groups, one led by Hissene Habré, a former FROLINAT leader, and the other by the then president, Goukouni Oueddei. Power shifted between the two until a truce was arranged in 1987, leaving Habré in control.

War broke out again in 1990 and Idriss Déby became president. The first multiparty elections were held in 1996. Fighting broke out again in the north in 1998, and continued in 2002.

Gambia, The

In 1965 it became independent and, in 1970, became a republic with Dawda Jawara as president. The government's main concerns were to develop tourism, which grew rapidly from the late 1970s, and relations with Senegal, which all but surrounds The Gambia. The two countries formed a treaty of association and, in 1978, the Gambian River Development Organization was formed. In 1982 the Confederation of Senegambia was set up. Both countries remained independent but shared military and financial resources. It ended in 1989.

In 1994 Jawara was deposed. Yahya Jammeh became head of a new new military government, which suspended all political activity. Civilian rule was restored in 1996. Jammeh continued as president and multiparty elections took place for a National Assembly. In 2001 Jammeh was re-elected president.

Awaiting evacuation
The people of Chad have experienced almost continual civil war since the country became independent in 1960. This illustration captures the moment when a victim of war receives water from an aid worker.

Sir Dawda Jawara
He was the longest-serving head of state in Gambia. A term served as prime minister from 1963–1970 was followed by a presidency which lasted from 1970–1994.

© DIAGRAM

Broken statue
Kwame Nkrumah, president of Ghana from 1960–1966, was overthrown in a military coup, a violent end reflected in this deliberate destruction.

Luiz Cabral
He was the first president of Guinea-Bissau in 1974 – when it gained its independence from Portugal – until 1981 when he was deposed.

Samuel Doe
He became head of state in Liberia in 1980 following a military coup. His assassination in 1990 led to an escalation in the 1989–1996 civil war

Ghana

In 1957 Ghana became the first black African colony to win its independence. Kwame Nkrumah became president in 1960 when Ghana became a republic. In 1964 Ghana became a one-party state. Nkrumah became increasingly authoritarian, and the economy suffered from falling prices and vast spending on development projects. In 1966 a military coup overthrew Nkrumah.

The country remained politically unstable until 1979 when Jerry Rawlings came to power. He introduced socialist policies to restore the economy, but was soon forced to introduce austerity measures. In 1991 the country returned to multiparty democracy with a new constitution modeled on that of the United States. Rawlings retired in 2000, and John Kufuor was elected president.

Guinea-Bissau

Following years of guerilla warfare, Guinea-Bissau achieved independence from Portugal in 1974. The first president was Luiz Cabral. In 1981 the prime minister, João Bernardo Viera, overthrew Cabral and set up a military revolutionary council with socialist policies.

Guinea-Bissau remained a one-party state until 1991. The first multiparty elections were held in 1994 and Viera was elected president. The economy was liberalized but the country remains poor and heavily dependent on foreign aid. In 1998-1999 troops from Senegal and Gambia entered the country to put down a military rebellion. Instability continued into the 21st century.

Liberia

Initially founded by Americans as a refuge for freed slaves, Liberia became independent in 1847, and has never been colonized. Its links with the US remain strong. During the first half of the 20th century, rubber production was the main industry, and the economy flourished. In the 1970s world rubber prices dropped. Food prices increased and there were riots in 1979.

In 1980 a military group seized power and their leader, Samuel Doe became head of state. Opponents of the government were killed or imprisoned. The economy was devastated by civil war, which lasted from 1989 until 1996. In 1997 Charles Taylor was elected president. There have been attempts to restore stability and rebuild the economy but, in 2000, the European Union (EU) suspended aid, accusing Liberia of assisting rebels in Sierra Leone. In 2002 a state of emergency was declared.

Sierra Leone

Colonized by Britain in 1787, Sierra Leone was originally a settlement for freed slaves. It achieved independence in 1961, and became a republic in 1971. In 1976 it became a one-party state.

During the 1990s civil war broke out and political instability intensified. Rebels from Liberia – the Revolutionary United Front (RUF) – invaded the country in 1990 with the aim of overthrowing the government. By the mid-1990s the RUF controlled many diamond-producing areas. In 1998 Nigerian troops intervened and overthrew the military regime. A peace agreement was signed, which was enforced by UN peacekeeping forces. Despite some further fighting, the war was officially declared over in 2002.

Togo

It became independent in 1960, with Sylvanus Olympio as the first president. Foreign investment was encouraged and phosphate became the country's main export.

In 1967 Gnassingbe Eyadéma seized power and ruled as a harsh dictator, making Togo a one-party state. Corruption and torture were common.

The economy began to decline in the 1980s, and there was social unrest. In 1991 political parties were made legal. Despite charges of fraud, Eyadéma was elected president in 1993, and again in 1998. In 1993 foreign aid was withdrawn because of mounting evidence of state terrorism. In 2000 a UN report alleged that Eyadéma, together with Blaise Compaoré, president of Burkina Faso, had aided the rebel group UNITA in Angola.

In 2001 an international commission stated human rights abuses had occurred during the 1998 elections.

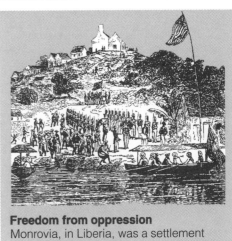

Freedom from oppression
Monrovia, in Liberia, was a settlement designed to house freed slaves from the US. In this illustration, the first president is shown arriving in 1849.

Ahmad Tejan Kabbah
He was elected prime minister of Sierra Leone in 1995, deposed in 1997, but returned from exile in 1998. Kabbah was reelected as president in 2002.

Gnassingbe Eyadéma
He became president of Togo following a bloodless coup in 1967. Although reelected under a new constitution in 1993, there have been many attempts to overthrow him.

© DIAGRAM

Former French West African colonies

Between 1895 and 1958, France controlled a huge area in West Africa, consisting of what are now Benin, Burkina Faso, Guinea, Ivory Coast, Mali, Mauritania, Niger, and Senegal. All, apart from Guinea (1958), achieved independent status in 1960.

Benin

Regional and political rivalries caused considerable social unrest in the years following independence. The first president was Hubert Maga. In 1972 Mathieu (later Ahmed) Kérékou came to power, remaining head of state until 1991. Dahomey was renamed the People's Republic of Benin; it became a one-party state, and, until 1989, communist policies were followed. In 1991 Benin became the first African nation to move from one party rule to multiparty democracy. Nicéphore Soglo, a former World Bank executive, was elected president. In 1996 Kérékou returned as president.

Burkina Faso

Burkina Faso remains one of the world's poorest countries. From 1966-1977 the country was under military rule. During the 1970s the country suffered inflation and drought in the Sahel, which led to starvation in the rural areas. Democracy was restored in 1977.

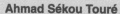

Thomas Sankara
He became prime minister of Burkina Faso in 1982, and president in 1983.

In 1982 Thomas Sankara came to power. Farming land was nationalized, and collectives set up. The country was renamed Burkina Faso ("the land of honest men") in 1984. With foreign aid, he initiated major projects, including mass vaccinations and tree planting to halt the spread of the Sahara. He was assassinated in 1987, and Blaise Campaoré came to power.

Ahmad Sékou Touré
He was the first president of an independent Guinea. His rule became increasingly oppressive in the 1970s and 1980s, and he died in 1984.

Guinea

The first president, Ahmad Sékou Touré, introduced socialist policies and made Guinea a one-party state. His rule became increasingly oppressive, and the country was criticized for its poor record on human rights. Conditions improved in the late 1970s when political prisoners were released, and the economy was partly liberalized.

A military council took power in 1984 and, by the 1990s, the economy was improving, due to measures imposed by the World Bank and International Monetary Fund (IMF). In 1991 the country returned to democracy. During the late 1990s refugees from Sierra Leone and Liberia flooded into the country, causing a crisis in 2001.

Ivory Coast

After independence, Ivory Coast became one of the most politically stable countries in Africa. The first president, Félix Houphouët-Boigny remained in office for 33 years until his death in 1993. An effective and pro-Western president, he maintained close links with France, so ensuring an export market for the country's cocoa and coffee.

For many years, the economy grew steadily and the country enjoyed prosperity. In recent years, the country has known some unrest. In 2002, an army mutiny against the government of Laurent Gbagbo led to civil war.

Our Lady of Peace
This basilica, situated in Ivory Coast, is the largest in the world.

Mali

The first president, Modibo Keita, made the country a socialist one-party state. Mali established links with Communist countries, moving away from France, its former colonial ruler. Little foreign aid entered the country. In 1968 a military regime was established. Moussa Traoré, worked to restore the country's finances but, during the 1970s, drought prevented progress.

In 1974 the country voted for a National Assembly and an elected president. In 1979, following the election, civilians entered the government. Increasing charges of government corruption caused unrest. In 1992 the first multiparty elections were held, and Alopha Oumar Konaré became Mali's first freely elected president.

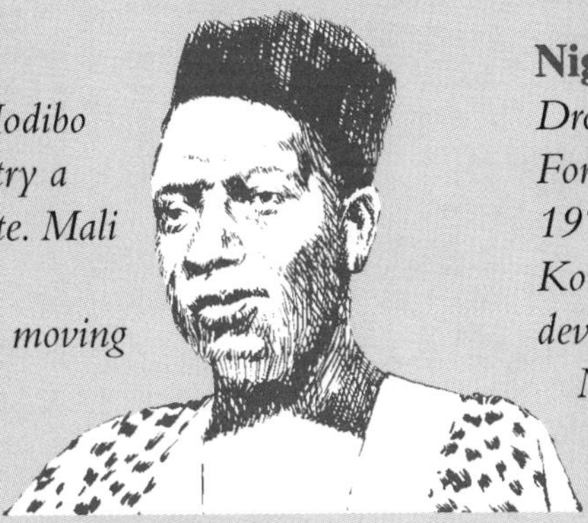

Modibo Keita
He became president of the Mali Federation, consisting of Senegal and French Soudan, in 1959.

Mauritania

A large country with a small population, Mauritania has experienced political instability and social tensions, particularly between Arab Moors, who dominate government, and black Africans in the south. Between 1974 and 1979 a war between Mauritania and Morocco over the Western Sahara also drained the country's resources.

In 1978 a military government was set up and, in 1991, Mauritania restored multiparty democracy.

Niger

Droughts hit Niger during the 1960s and 1970s. Foreign aid flooded in but was misappropriated. In 1974 the military took control and under Seyni Kountché began a program of agricultural development. French aid was used to develop Niger's uranium deposits, which became the country's chief export.

In 1991 a new constitution was introduced for multiparty elections. Between 1991 and 1997 Tuareg separatists in the north rebelled. Although multiparty democracy was suspended briefly, it was restored in 1999.

Senegal

Since independence, Senegal has become more politically stable and wealthier than many other countries in the region. It has maintained close links with France and for forty years, until 2000, was a socialist state.

During the 1980s, Senegal formed a confederation with Gambia, but it was abandoned in 1989. In 1990 there were border clashes with Mauritania in the north. In 2000 Abdoulaye Wade became president of the country.

Léopold Senghor
He became the first president of Senegal in 1960, and remained in power until his eventual resignation from office in 1981.

Moktar Ould Daddah
The first president of an independent Mauritania (1960–1978), he worked to unify his ethnically divided people but was eventually overthrown. He is shown here with General de Gaulle of France.

© DIAGRAM

Nigeria

With a population of nearly 127 million people (2000), Nigeria is the most populated country in West Africa. It is home to more than 200 ethnic groups. With its rich petroleum, gas and mineral reserves, it should be a wealthy country, but a series of military coups and ethnic conflicts have weakened the country over a period of time.

Nigeria became independent from Britain in 1960. Differences between leaders of Nigeria's rival ethnic groups had already caused problems. To ensure that major ethnic groups were represented, the country was divided into three regions: a northern, mainly Muslim, area where the Hausa were the leading group; a western region where the Yoruba lived; and an eastern area, where the Igbo (or Ibo) formed the main group. In 1963 Nigeria became a federal republic. In 1966 Nigeria's first prime minister was killed in a military coup. The military leader was an Igbo, who ended the federal system and appointed many Igbos to high office, which led to riots in the north.

L'EXPRESS

BIAFRA: LA FIN

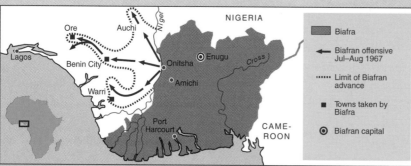

The end of the war, 1970 (above)
The cover of a French magazine announces the end of the war between Nigeria and the Republic of Biafra. The Biafrans were finally starved into submission after a bitter and bloody conflict which lasted for two and a half years.

The Biafran War (left)
The war lasted from July 1967 until January 1970. The map (top left) shows the territory claimed by Biafra, and its offensives in 1967; the map (bottom left) focuses on the territory reclaimed by Nigeria, and its counteroffensives, in 1970.

The Biafran War

In 1966 General Gowon took power and divided Nigeria into 12 states. The following year, Odumegwu Ojukwu, military governor of the eastern region, proclaimed the eastern region an independent republic called Biafra. Reasons given for the breakaway were that the Igbo feared political domination by the northern region (many thousands had already been murdered), and also the discovery of oil in the region.

Civil war broke out in 1967. Nigeria hoped to stop the secession quickly but, in fact, the war lasted for two and a half years, and it was extremely bitter. Initially the Biafrans were successful but, by December 1969, Nigerian troops had reduced Biafra to a small area. Nigerians cut off food supplies so many Biafrans were starved into submission. They surrendered in 1970.

Oil, politics, and human rights

Oil exports boomed in the 1970s, but political problems continued. Gowon was deposed in 1975. His successor was killed in 1976, and was followed by Olesegun Obasanjo, who ended military rule. The elected president was deposed in 1983 and another military regime was installed.

In 1993 General Abacha seized power, and it was not until after his death in 1998 that civilian rule was finally restored. In 1995 Nigeria was expelled from the Commonwealth and the government was accused of violating international human rights when Ogoni activists were accused of plotting to overthrow it. Despite international protests, eight were executed, including the Nigerian writer Ken Saro-Wiwa. In 2002 a lawsuit was brought, charging the oil company Shell with complicity.

Civilian rule was restored in 1998. Olesegun Obasanjo was elected president, by which time Nigeria had been divided into 36 states. Ethnic conflict continued into the early 2000s, with Christian-Muslim clashes in the north, and Hausa-Yoruba conflict in the southwest.

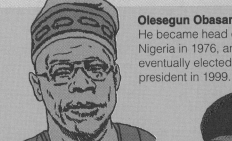

Olesegun Obasanjo (left)
He became head of state in Nigeria in 1976, and was eventually elected as president in 1999.

Fighting for a cause
This Igbo man is one of many thousands of soldiers who fought for freedom from Nigerian control during the Biafran War (1967–1970).

Sanni Abacha (right)
He became head of Nigeria's military government in 1993, and served in this position until his death in 1998.

© DIAGRAM

Coups d'État in West Africa

Independence from colonial rule by European powers proved difficult to achieve for many African nations. Yet, once independence had been achieved, problems beset the new states.

As the maps (right) show, some nations were subject to political instability and frequent military *coups d'état* after independence. The region of West Africa has experienced nearly 40 *coups* in the last 40 years, with Benin alone enduring five of them.

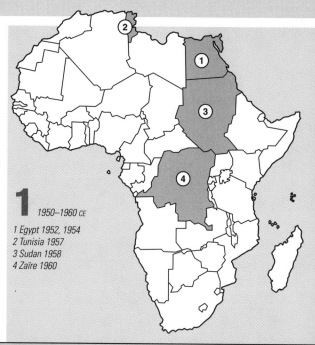

1 1950–1960 CE

1 Egypt 1952, 1954
2 Tunisia 1957
3 Sudan 1958
4 Zaïre 1960

West African *coups d'état*

These are some of the leaders of 20th century *coups d'état* in West Africa.

Mathieu Ahmed Kérékou
He became president of Dahomey (now Benin) in 1972 following a coup.

Jerry Rawlings
He seized power in Ghana in 1979, and again in 1981, before finally being elected as the president in 1992.

Moussa Traoré
He became head of state in Mali in 1968 after a coup in which Modibo Keita was deposed. A later coup in 1991 deposed him.

Blaise Compaoré
He became president of Burkina Faso in 1987 following a coup in which he deposed his former friend, Thomas Sankara.

Lansana Conté
He seized power in Guinea in 1984 after leading a bloodless coup following the death of Sékou Touré.

Sanni Abacha
He seized power in 1993 in Nigeria, and then became head of the military government there.

Félix Malloum
He became leader of the Supreme Military Council following a coup ousting President Tombalbaye in Chad in 1975.

Samuel Doe
He seized power in Liberia in 1980 following a military coup but, in 1990, was assassinated.

Gnassingbe Eyadéma
He seized power in Togo in 1967 in a bloodless coup, and later became its president.

2 *1961–1970 CE*

1 Benin 1963, 1965, 1967, 1969
2 Congo 1963, 1968
3 Togo 1963, 1967
4 Sudan 1964, 1969
5 Algeria 1965
6 Burundi 1965, 1966
7 Central African Republic 1965
8 Zaïre 1965
9 Burkina Faso 1966
10 Ghana 1966
11 Nigeria 1966
12 Uganda 1966
13 Sierra Leone 1967, 1968

14 Mali 1968
15 Libya 1969
16 Somalia 1969
17 Lesotho 1970

3 *1971–1980 CE*

1 Uganda 1971, 1979
2 Benin 1972
3 Ghana 1972, 1978, 1979
4 Madagascar 1972
5 Rwanda 1973
6 Ethiopia 1974
7 Niger 1974
8 Chad 1975
9 Nigeria 1975
10 Burundi 1976
11 Congo 1977
12 Seychelles 1977
13 Comoros 1978
14 Mauritania 1978, 1980

15 Equatorial Guinea1979
16 Burkina Faso 1980
17 Central African Republic 1980
18 Guinea-Bissau 1980
19 Liberia 1980

4 *1981–1990 CE*

1 Central African Republic 1981
2 Ghana 1981
3 Chad 1982
4 Burkina Faso 1983, 1987
5 Nigeria 1983
6 Guinea 1984
7 Mauritania 1984
8 Sudan 1985, 1989
9 Uganda 1985
10 Lesotho 1986
11 Burundi 1987
12 Tunisia 1987

13 Somalia 1990

5 *1991–2000 CE*

1 Ethiopia 1991
2 Lesotho 1991, 1993
3 Mali 1991
4 Algeria 1992
5 Chad 1992
6 Sierra Leone 1992, 1997
7 Nigeria 1993
8 Gambia 1994
9 Burundi 1996
10 Niger 1996, 1999
11 Congo, Dem Rep 1997
12 Congo, Republic of 1997
13 Comoros 1999

14 Guinea-Bissau 1999
15 Ivory Coast 1999

Glossary

abolition The act of abolishing, or doing away with, something. Historically, abolition has been used to refer to the abolition of slavery and the slave trade.

adobe Sun-dried brick used for building, and the material used to make such bricks.

amazon In ancient Greek mythology, one of a race of female warriors who lived near the Black Sea. More generally, any tall, strong, and aggressive woman. See *gbeto* below.

BCE Before Common Era.

birane The Hausa name for a walled town.

burial mound In West Africa, historic human-made structures that were built over the graves of notables. These large earthen mounds often contain grave goods.

cash crops Crops, such as cotton, coffee, and cocoa, that are grown to sell for money rather than to be eaten by the grower and family.

CE Common Era.

colony A territory occupied by a ruling state.

confederation A united group of, for example, nations, formed for the benefit of all members.

Creoles A Liberian élite that evolved from generations of intermarriage between Africans, Europeans, and freed slaves.

district officers Colonial officials, generally Europeans, who linked local regions to the central government.

divine king A king who is believed to be a god on earth, a representative or god on earth, or a person given the right to rule by a god. Historically, many West African kings were divine kings. Their health and wellbeing was believed to be linked to that of their kingdom.

dynasty A succession of rulers who claim descent from a common ancestor.

élite A group with access to power because of its social standing, wealth, or education.

empire A major political unit with a large territory, generally containing a number of smaller territories.

fama The ruler of a town in the Mali empire. The position was inherited.

gbeto The oldest amazon unit in the Dahomey army.

ghana The Soninke word for "king" or "war-chief." The Soninke people live in what is now central Mali.

habe The king of a Hausa *birane*.

Islam Religion practiced the world over in which Allah is God, and Muhammad is his prophet. Followers of this religion are called Muslims.

jihad Holy war launched by Muslims against nonbelievers, or for principles and beliefs.

kafu The basic political unit among the Mande people of ancient Mali. A *kafu* is a community of one or several thousand people living in, or near, a town ruled by a *fama*.

kangbodé Second minister to the Dahomey king in what is now Benin.

kora A harplike musical instrument from West Africa; the most common have 21 strings.

mansa Title of the king of ancient Mali.

millennium One thousand years.

Muslim A follower of Islam.

mya Millions of years ago.

nationalist A member of a political party or group arguing for independence or strong national government.

nomad A person who does not live in one place but travels, generally with the seasons, in search of fresh water and pasture for their herds of animals, and often within a fixed area.

ogiso Benin (southeastern Nigeria) was made up of several former villages, each with its own head. The *ogiso* was the head of all these chiefs.

ohemma Title of the most senior Asante woman (Ghana).

oni Title of the king of the Yoruba kingdom of Ife, in what is now southeastern Nigeria.

pastoralists People who live by raising animals.

pilgrimage A journey made for religious reasons.

queen mother A position of great honor given to the most senior women in Asante and Fon society, and in historic Benin.

savanna Tropical grasslands with scattered shrubs and a few thorny trees.

sultan Title of the king of a Muslim state called a sultanate.

tononu The most important minister to the king of Dahomey; he was the king's mouthpiece.

uzama ogiso Title of village chiefs in Benin.

vassal state A tributary state.

Bibliography

Ajayi, J. F. Ade, and Crowder, M., *The History of West Africa,* 2nd ed. Harlow (UK): Longman (1976)

Ajayi, J. F. Ade, and Crowder, M., *Historical Atlas of Africa,* Cambridge (UK): Cambridge University Press (1985)

Awooner, Kofi, *Ghana: a Political History,* Accra, Ghana: Sedco Publishing Ltd. & Woeli Publishing Services (1990)

Ayensu, Edward S., *Ashanti Gold,* Accra, Ghana: Ashanti Goldfields Company Limited (1997)

Barnett, Jeanie M., *Ghana,* Broomall, Pa.: Chelsea House Publishers (1997)

Beckwith, Carol, and Tepelit Ole Saitoti, *Maasai,* London: Abradale (1993)

Beckwith, Carol and van Offellen, Marion, *Nomads of Niger,* New York: Harry N. Abrams Inc. (1983)

Boone, S. A., *Radiance from the Waters: Ideals of Feminine Beauty in Mende Art,* New Haven, CT.: Yale University Press (1986)

Catchpole, B. and Akinjogbin, I. A., *A History of West Africa in Maps and Diagrams,* London: Collins (1992)

Clifford, Mary Louise, I. A., *The Land and People of Liberia,* Philadelphia: Lippincott (1971)

Connah, G., *African Civilisations,* Cambridge (UK): Cambridge University Press (1987)

Crowder, Michael, *West Africa: an Introduction to its History,* Harlow (UK): Longman (1977)

Davidson, Basil, *A History of West Africa,* Harlow (UK): Longman (1977)

Diagram Group, *African History On File,* New York: Facts On File (2003)

Diagram Group, *Encyclopedia of African Nations,* New York: Facts On File (2002)

Diagram Group, *Encyclopedia of African Peoples,* New York: Facts On File (2000)

Diagram Group, *Peoples of West Africa,* New York: Facts On File (1997)

Diagram Group, *Religions On File,* New York: Facts On File (1990)

Diagram Group, *Timelines On File,* 4 vols. New York: Facts On File (2000)

Fynn, J. K., *Asante and its Neighbors,* Evanston, Ill.: Northwestern University Press (1971)

Gibbs Jr, J. ed., *Peoples of Africa,* New York: Holt, Rinehart & Winston (1965)

Harrison Church, R. J., *West Africa,* 8th ed. Harlow (UK): Longman (1980)

Haskins, J. and Biondi, J., *From the Afar to the Zulu,* New York: Walker Publishing Co. (1995)

Hiskett, M., *The Development of Islam in West Africa,* Harlow (UK): Longman (1984)

Massing, A., *The Economic History of the Kru,* Stutttgart: Franz Steiner (1980)

Oshomha, I., *The Ibo of East Central Nigeria,* Ibadan, Nigeria: New Era Publishers (1990)

Wiseman, J.A., *Political Leaders in Black Africa,* Brookfield, VT.: Edward Elgar Publishing Co. (1991)

Index

Index

Index